From Raj To Riches

From Raj To Riches

Overcoming Life Through Faith

by
Ernest L. Thomas

ISBN: 978-0-692-86005-2

For booking, personal appearances and interviews

email address e@ernestlthomas.com
website www.ernestlthomas.com
P.O. Box 11533 Glendale, CA 91226

Dedication

This book is dedicated, above all, to the only father I've known, my heavenly Father — Jehovah — and to my Lord and Savior — Jesus Christ. To my best friend and mother, Liza Latham; my grandmother, Lizzie Miller; my baby brother, Anton Thomas, aka Toni Sue Farrell; and the greatest — Muhammad Ali, I love you forever.

Acknowledgements

Thank you, Lord God, for establishing divine connections in my life with those who have helped to make this book possible in some form or fashion. To Prophet Brian Turner, the miracle of West Angeles and a great man of God, thank you for your support and guidance. To Laval Belle, the reason this book is finally a reality, I can't thank you enough for believing that this would be an impactful and meaningful project worth pursuing. To Lisa Beasley, my editor, who said that it was an honor to meet me and that she's always been a fan. After talking and working with you for many hours, I am now a fan of yours. You went beyond the job of editor. I felt your passion and love for my story and your understanding of what this book is about. I thank God for putting us together, and I look forward to completing many more projects with you. To Carolyn Billups and Cynthia Busby, thank you for helping to get the story down. To Sharon Gardner, my ride-or-die, thank you for your love and support and your help with this book. I love you forever.

Thank you to my pastor, Bishop Blake, and my West Angeles Church of God in Christ family for your love. Bishop Blake, I thank you for your encouragement and for speaking profound words into my life. Yes, I do expect a miracle!

To Malik Kalonji, thank you for being there during the worst of my storms. I will never forget your love and support.

To Kevin Carter and Eric Bowman, true men of God, I thank you for your friendship and your dedication to the calling on your lives to help our communities. To Jean-Claude La Marre and Yolanda Buggs, the early champions of my autobiography, I will be forever grateful for your encouraging words. Thank you, Jake Smith, for your vision. Without you, I wouldn't have a book. Thank you for believing even more than I did. To my dear friend and college roommate Rick Nichols, thank you for over fifty years of friendship. Thank you to my dear friend Tanya Sanchez and my daughter, Pam Trotter, for always loving and supporting me.

There are so many other family and friends I want to acknowledge, but that would be a book in and of itself. To all those I didn't mention, know that I love you with all my heart, and I am thankful to God for creating a place in my life for you. I am eternally grateful.

Table of Contents

CHAPTER ONE

GARY, INDIANA

I was born in Gary, Indiana, on March 26, 1949. I am truly a miracle because my mother tried to abort me. My aunt and my grandmother found her in the bathroom with a coat hanger that a friend of hers had told her would work. My mom said my grandmother and aunt threatened to give her the whipping of her life, and she was grateful they did because she was going to do it for sure. She had already given birth to my sister two years earlier, and she didn't want to go through that pain ever again. My mother's landlady told her to name me Ernest. It was the name of her landlady's late husband. So, my mother named me Ernest, and I can honestly say that the name has brought me good fortune and even fame.

My sister, Rosie, was born in Sikeston, Missouri. Her father's name was Robert Thomas. He was known as a "Romeo" who loved women. My uncles beat him up and made him marry Mom. According to my mother, Robert was a nice guy, and he never hit her. But he was always cheating. This led mom to have an affair with a man named William Berry. He was a handsome guy that she showed interest in only to get back at Robert, but she got pregnant with me in the process.

Soon after Mom got pregnant, she moved to Gary to be with my grandmother. My aunt was in intensive care, and Grandma wanted to be there for her. Shortly after I was born, my father attempted to see me. He called my mother and asked if he could come and see his son. My grandmother viewed William and Robert as playboys who weren't serious about marriage, love, or children. So she told my mom to tell William he wasn't needed — that she would take care of me. And that's what she did.

Robert was always in Rosie's life, calling periodically, and he came to visit her in Gary once. Recently, my mother revealed to me that Robert had always believed I was his son. She was still married to him when she had the affair with William, so he went to his grave thinking that I was his son. I asked Mom if it was possible that Robert could be my father, but she said absolutely not. But, for some reason, even when I became a teenager, Mom never wanted me to meet William Berry. When I was a baby, my mother and grandmother feared he might kidnap me. But even while I was in high school and college they prevented him from meeting me. When I was in college, a friend of my mother's told me that she had my father's number, but when I called her later to get it, she told me she couldn't give it to me. I knew Mom had talked to her and told her not to give me the information. As I've moved on into my senior years, Mom recently said to me one day, "You should find your father." *Really, Mom?* Gotta love her. But it's all still a mystery to me. Maybe one day I'll go to Sikeston and see if this man even existed at all.

When I was eleven years old, my mother gave birth to my brother, Anton, on Thanksgiving Day. He looked like a white baby, with reddish-blond hair. His father, Samuel Steele, was a good man, and he and his brothers always made themselves available to Anton.

Out of all my relatives, the one I most admire is my great-grandfather Jake Sledge. He was a Freemason, and his nickname was Mister Millionaire, because he always had money, land, and livestock. During the Great Depression, he loaned money to White and Black people. One of them gave him the name Mister Millionaire. After enduring a heavy battle with alcohol, he became a born-again Christian. My grandmother was just like her father. She always had money under her mattress or in her brazier or in some other secret place. They knew how to handle money.

All my uncles worshipped the ground I walked on, especially the twins, Uncle Wiley and Uncle Riley. They never spanked me. They never yelled at me. They adored everything about me. Uncle Wiley would always tell me, "You like to not been here. I saved your life." One day, while he was taking my mother to the doctor when she was pregnant with me, they were rear-ended by a car. Uncle Wiley said he had to rush my mother to the doctor so she wouldn't lose me. And because he was driving, of course, he saved my life.

Not having the presence of a father in my life, I was very attached to my mother and grandmother. So, when it came time to start kindergarten, I didn't want to go. I didn't want to leave the warm environment, good food, and unconditional love I received in the comforts of home. So, I went kicking and screaming all the way. I remember standing at the screen door in our home in the Dorie Miller Projects, begging my mother and grandmother to let me stay home. They assured me that I would love school, and they would be waiting for me when school let out. Then my mother took me by the hand and walked me to school.

When I saw the teacher, my fear subsided. She was this beautiful, tall angel, wearing a champagne dress, with long legs that went on forever. She had the most beautiful face I'd ever seen. I didn't mind being in kindergarten anymore. She knew I was afraid, so she was extra kind and very sweet. I can't remember anything about kindergarten except the champagne dress, her smell, her beautiful face, and how nice she was to me.

Ms. Thomas, my sixth grade teacher, was also unforgettable. But it was not her looks that made her unforgettable; it was her love for teaching and her faith in my abilities as a student. She had this dynamic, charismatic personality, but she was like a drill sergeant. She was a sorority lady — a Delta Sigma Theta sister — and she had a paddle on the wall with the Delta Sigma Theta insignia on it. And, boy, when she was upset or felt you weren't giving your all, she could swing that paddle! Before spanking me, she would say: "Boy, don't you know you can do anything? Don't you know that I'm not going to allow you to fail?" She would grab me at the back of my pants and tighten them. Then she would start swinging that paddle like there was no tomorrow. I usually got the spankings because I played hooky, not because I didn't apply myself in school. I didn't tell my grandmother about the spankings because she didn't allow me or my siblings to get spanked, ever. And I know Grandmother would have come to that school and jumped on Ms. Thomas.

The other children were jealous of me because they thought I "talked White," but I was simply imitating Ms. Thomas' speech pattern. To them, I was talking like a White person and acting like I thought I was better than they were. But what really pushed them over the edge was when Ms. Thomas designated me to write down the name of anyone who talked while she left the class. Because I was a Christian and was trying to be like Jesus, I never wanted to lie. I wrote down everybody's name, because everybody talked. So, when it was time to go home, the boys in the class said to me, "You're going to get your butt whipped today." I can still remember their faces even though it was over fifty years ago. The ring leader was the one I remember most. He was a light-skinned guy with "good hair." Light skin was worshipped in those days.

The boys caught me and smacked me around. I felt so belittled and ashamed because it was my own people who were doing this to me. And because I didn't want to feel like that again, I skipped school for two weeks and went to the soda shop instead. I didn't go to the soda shop every day. But I went three to four times each week.

At the end of the second week, the principal called my mother and grandmother and told them what I had been doing. After hearing why I had been skipping school, my mother said to me, "God will understand if you don't tell the truth in order to save a life." Then she gave me an example: "If I had an angry, abusive boyfriend who came to our house and didn't know I was there, and he asked if I was home, you wouldn't tell the truth, because I could be put in danger and even killed." And then I understood.

While growing up in Gary, there weren't any race problems that I can recall. But the South was another story entirely. Every summer, we visited Aunt Betty in Tunica, Mississippi. It was especially traumatic for me when Emmett Till was brutally murdered. I still remember his face — bashed beyond recognition, even to his mother, by two White men who were acquitted of the murder by an all-White jury. They later admitted killing him to *Look* magazine, knowing they couldn't be tried twice for a murder they had been acquitted of. They said they had planned to beat him up, but they didn't intend to kill him. But when he boasted of having a White girlfriend, they decided to murder him. I can still see the photo of his face in the casket in *Jet* magazine. My mother and grandmother would show the photo to me and my sister over and over again, warning us that this would happen to us if we didn't say "yes, sir" or "no, sir" and "yes, ma'am" or "no, ma'am" to any White person we met in the South, even the children. Emmett Till was fourteen years old, younger than I was at the time it happened. Every time I think about that photo, waves of fear still haunt me, even to this day.

I experienced blatant, unapologetic, and ugly racism for the first time in Clarendon, Arkansas. I was eight years old at the time. I went with my uncle, who was going there to attend the funeral of his wife's brother. We went to a restaurant, along with his wife and a few of her relatives, and this White woman told us to go to the back. "Why are we going to back?" I asked my uncle. He said, "Be quiet, boy. You'll get us killed." We went to the back where there was a wooden counter and old chairs, and we sat there and ordered our food. There was a yellow and white cat in the corner eating. I remember these white and red silk curtains that separated us from the white patrons. I could hear the sound of glasses, plates, and silverware clinking together and people laughing and having a good time. That was the only time in my life that I wanted to be White. I prayed to God that night to please make me White so that I would never have to experience that again.

Some of the most difficult early memories I have are of the abuse I saw my mother suffer. I remember having a red fire truck, and I remember this giant man beating on my mother as she screamed for help, which I was too young to give her. All I remember was screaming and crying, wanting him to stop, and then my mind went blank. Several years later, I was riding with my mom and her fiancé, J.C., and they got into an argument. He started hitting her. I started crying, and I told him to stop. He told me to shut up, and I felt there was nothing I could do to help her that time either. In all fairness, my mother was always saying things to instigate the arguing and fighting because she was jealous or she wanted attention. She'd throw a hit, and they'd punch right back. Only they kept on hitting because the thought of being hit by a woman angered them.

I tried my best to destroy my mother's relationship with J.C. I told her that he had tuberculosis and he would kill us all if she married him. I felt he would destroy the entire family, because when he hit Mom he was the enemy. But the fighting stopped after their first two years together.

One night I decided to kill him because I was just tired of him hitting my mother. I got a butcher knife from the kitchen. I went into the bedroom where they were sleeping. I was going to aim the butcher knife right at his chest. Fortunately, my mother woke up and saw me. She pleaded with me not to kill him. He lay there sound asleep while my mother begged for his life. She said, "You know God wouldn't want you to do that." So I didn't. But my cousin Sidney found out about the incident, and that was a game changer. Sidney was like Shaft and the Godfather in our community, and he didn't take any flack from anybody! He came over later that morning and said, "Where's J.C.?" He had a gun, and he pointed it right at J.C.'s head and said, "Nigga, do you want to die?" J.C. pleaded with him not to kill him. It was a fact that Sidney had killed people before, and I knew he would kill J.C. But in that moment I realized I didn't want J.C. to die. I pleaded with Sidney not to kill him. My sister did, too. He finally lowered the gun and said, "Don't you ever put your hands on my cousin again!" And J.C. never did. I thought I wanted to kill J.C., but I realized that I did love him. But my anger overshadowed it. That was my mama, and I had to protect her. But I couldn't kill anybody. I realized that, too.

J.C., I'm happy to say, was my mother's soul mate for thirty-five years. I never saw a man so devoted to a woman in my life. Mom probably did start those fights with him, and he reacted like a typical male would, and struck back. During the thirty-five years they were together, they were only apart for two days. That was when he went to his sister's funeral. I was grateful to see my mother truly happy.

Some of the best memories I have from my childhood are of having the Christmas plays and celebrating the Christmas season. I remember one particular play, *Scrooge*, starring Robert Riley. Oh, my God! He was so brilliant. He looked like a lighter-skinned version of Fred Berry—Rerun. He could sing, he could dance, and he could act. And as I sat there in awe of him, I said to myself, *"I could never do that"* because I felt I was too shy.

But I got my first taste of acting when I was in the ninth grade, at Pulaski Junior High, even though I wasn't aware of it at the time. In my speech class, we had to do a persuasive speech about something we were against. So I (the church boy) chose legalization of marijuana. I did all my research, and I went to podium. I felt at home. I became another person. I gave my speech with conviction, and the teacher was looking at me in amazement. I gave all the benefits of marijuana and all the reasons why it should be legalized. I was on a great high that I couldn't explain. I shot down all other arguments, and I was smiling with a knowingness and confidence I had never felt before. I didn't want it to end. I loved being right and in charge. That's what I felt: RIGHT and IN CHARGE.

Going home that day, I kept hearing my speech and seeing the faces of all my opponents. I had shut them down with facts and counterarguments. I was on that high all night and for many days later.

My second persuasive speech involved convincing the class that the Islam was the right religion, and they should all join. I did my research, and I even went to the temple with J.C.'s cousin. He knew I was COGIC (Church of God in Christ), but he didn't attack my faith. He invited me openly and respectfully, and I went.

When I presented *this* speech in class, I—this young, COGIC church boy—got up to the podium and was even more confident than I had been before. I wish I had a tape of both of those speeches. But I remember how I felt. I was on top of the world. I shut down all arguments and responded to all questions. The teacher told me she saw something that she had never seen in me before. My speech made the students emotional and even angry and frustrated, because I had the answers. Right or wrong, I had an answer for everything. It was a supernatural high that I never wanted to end.

Another foreshadowing of my acting gift took place in history class. I had to recite the *Gettysburg Address*. The teacher said I recited it as if I was there. He said it was weird, but he liked it. And the class stared at me like I was weirdo. My teacher said it seemed as though I had taken on an older spirit as I recited the speech.

Other indications of my gift came while reading. I always became a part of the world and the time period in which the book was set. I could smell the porridge or soup, the house, and the yard, and I could see the action with my imagination. The stories came alive in my mind. I believe all these things were gifts from God, preparing me for the acting profession.

My imagination served me well when I wrote a story titled *The Black Prince*. My English teacher loved it and asked me how I arrived at the plot. I actually don't remember. It was just something that was inside of me, and I obeyed and expressed it. I didn't keep a copy, which I regret. But, even then, God was preparing me for a life as a creator, actor, artist, and writer.

My teachers told my mother that I was a great student, but I tended to drift off and arbitrarily look out the window like I wasn't there. I must admit, I have always felt like I was out of place in my family and in society. The only place I felt connected was in my relationship with God. I enjoyed church, I loved praying, and I loved gospel songs. I have never been afraid to die, because I know I will be home with Jesus when I do. And what could be better than that? I totally accepted Jesus as my Savior who died on the cross for me, and I have been connected to that Creator all my life, even when I stopped going to church while I was in college. I even became an atheist for a moment, but Christ brought me back.

After graduating from Pulaski Junior High, I was selected, along with a few other Black students, to integrate an all-White high school—Emerson High. The White parents greeted us with signs saying "Go back to Africa" and many other negative things about Black people. So, I went there, but I was afraid. I still remembered Emmett Till. But I never had any fights with the White students. Now, don't get me wrong; there were fights among Black and White students, but they were few. And I realize that it was a good thing that we were forced to face each other and realize that we had more in common than we had differences. But one thing that really struck me was when a history teacher had to be reprimanded for stating in her class that Black people hadn't contributed anything great to our history—period.

But then there were other teachers. What I loved most about Emerson High School was one teacher in particular — Ms. Nichols, a southern White woman from Tennessee. She was our high school music teacher. She was so loving, so sweet, and she really made me fall even more in love with music. I'm not a great singer, but I can sing, and I found that out through the efforts of Ms. Nichols. She said I had a beautiful tenor voice, and she put me in the school choir.

For as long as I can remember, music has been like a gift from heaven to me. Music has always given me peace of mind, soothed my soul, lifted my spirit, and offered me hope. I remember listening to Mahaila Jackson a lot when I was growing up. My grandmother listened to her all the time. Her soulful spirit and beautiful voice was a true source of peace and hope.

Now, during that time, it was a sin, according to my church, to listen to secular music, but I cheated sometimes. I loved all the Motown artists — Diana Ross and the Supremes, the Marvelettes, the Temptations, Smokey Robinson and the Miracles, and the Four Tops, just to name a few. I discovered the sounds of Motown when I stayed with my cousins at my Aunt Gussie's house on the weekends. There was no church music blaring over there! There was plenty of partying and laughing, and people having a good time. I remember watching my aunt's older sons slow dancing with girls in the neighborhood to the song "You Really Got a Hold on Me" by Smokey Robinson and the Miracles. Smokey has always been one of my favorite singers of all time. And I was in love with Diana Ross. I remember watching her perform on *The Ed Sullivan Show* with the Supremes. I thought she was so beautiful. We actually have the same birthday, so I felt we had a special connection.

Another one of my favorites was Aretha Franklin. When she sang gospel music, she made you want to shout, and when she sang secular songs, she made you want to party. Whenever I heard "Respect," I always tried to resist moving my feet, but I could never resist. I had been born again, into Aretha Franklin. But it was clear that the song wasn't dirty or nasty. It was about love. But I always felt guilty, and guilt plagued me most of my life.

I believe most of the guilt I felt stemmed from the strict guidelines of the COGIC/Pentecostal faith. However, when I descended into what felt like hell itself, doing drugs and partying, that faith saved my life. According to my church, it was a sin to go to the movies, watch television, or attend dances. Anything that was considered secular or was associated with being among unbelievers, unless it involved preaching or ministering to them, was a sin. I never told my pastor or the missionaries about my love for secular music, but I talked to God about it, and I never thought or felt that he disapproved of it.

I also enjoyed watching television. I loved the comedies, and my grandmother watched television with me sometimes. She loved only one show, *The Tom Jones Show*, and, man, he could sing! My mother, on the other hand, never watched television and never went to the movies. But she was always full of laughter—always happy. My mother has the greatest laugh. It sounds like the entire room is laughing when she laughs. She would always say, "Because of the love of Jesus Christ, I don't need anything to entertain me." That was truly amazing to me.

I also enjoyed going to the movies. But I kept my movie-going a secret. When I went to see *The Ten Commandments*, I felt the church would be happy about it. But when I went to church the following Sunday and told them I had gone to see it, you would have thought I had told them I had gone to see the devil himself because they were so upset to discover that I had been "sitting among the heathens." So, I decided going to the movies would continue to be my little secret.

Because I could never speak to anyone about television, music, or movies, I was a loner. My mother's friends would tell her to make me go outside and interact with the other kids. But I told my mother that I couldn't play with other kids unless they were members of the Church of God in Christ. She told me to go out there and be nice. So I would always minister to them and let them know that I was praying for them to get saved. They had to get saved in my church because COGIC was the only true church. That's what we believed at that time. But as time went on, we stopped believing that way.

My first movie star crush was on Geraldine Page. I went to see her in *Summer and Smoke*, based on the play written by Tennessee Williams. I didn't understand what was happening in the movie, but I could feel something. I felt her tears. I felt her emotions. I didn't understand what was going on, but I remember realizing I was in love with her. She touched me and brought something to life in me, which were probably the seeds of my passion for acting. I don't know. But I remember that day like it was yesterday. When I left the theater, I didn't walk home; I floated.

I suffered with asthma until I was eighteen. So, I spent a lot of time in bed. This allowed me to enjoy a lot of comedies. *I Love Lucy* was my favorite, but I also loved *My Little Margie, The Danny Thomas Show, The Andy Griffith Show, The Mickey Mouse Club, Rin Tin Tin, The Lone Ranger, Cisco Kid, Broken Arrow, Gunsmoke, The Rifle Man, Johnny Yuma, Wanted Dead or Alive, Have Gun Will Travel, Wagon Train, The Perry Mason Show, Ed Sullivan, The Dick van Dyke Show, Amos and Andy,* and *Captain Kangaroo.* Although the comedies were my favorites, I also loved the westerns. I would always ask my mother to give me cowboy hats and guns for Christmas. I loved John Wayne, and I wanted to be a cowboy like all the cowboys I saw on television.

When I watched these shows, my imagination took me right into the heart of the story and into the characters. I could even smell things I saw on television. It was really a surreal experience for me.

Suffering with asthma got severe at times, and none of the medicine seemed to help when it did. I remember one night, in particular. It was late, and everyone was asleep. I was wheezing so badly that I got up and went to the living room and sat on the floor, by the couch. I said, "God, please, please take me now. I just don't want to suffer like this, Lord. Please take me, Jesus." My grandmother and mother heard my prayer and were so alarmed by it that they begged me to never pray that prayer again. I told them that we're going to Jesus anyway, and I was ready to go. My mother said, "Jesus wants you to live and enjoy life." I could tell they were really worried, so I never prayed that prayer again. But God knew that I was ready to go if he would take me.

Although God didn't heal me that night, I have witnessed his miraculous healing power. One instance I remember vividly took place at Gospel Temple Church of God in Christ. We were having Bible class that evening. Missionary Taylor was there, and she was sick with pneumonia or the flu. When Bible class was about over, she asked Elder Chandler if she could pray with all the children in the church. There weren't many of us, maybe six. When she came to me, I prayed, "Please heal Missionary Taylor, Lord, in Jesus' name." I kept praying, and she started dancing and shouting. All her coughing and sneezing went away. "This child has the gift of healing! God has given this child the gift of healing!" she exclaimed. I was scared to death. I was glad she was healed, but I didn't want to hear that I had the gift. I think it was mainly because I didn't want to experience the jealousy of others again. But Elder Chandler always singled me out. He came to the front of the church and said, "What God has placed in Ernest L. Thomas no man can take from him." Well, that did it. None of the kids liked me after that. Missionary Taylor declared I had the gift of healing, and I just wanted to forget she had ever said it.

It seemed like we were always in church—twice on Sundays, Bible study during the week, revivals in neighboring cities, like Chicago. There was always church somewhere, and we were often right there. I remember when they used to have all the children sitting at the altar, praying for the Holy Spirit. I also remember feeling the fullness of God in me. We were at that altar for hours it seemed. I remember the missionaries praying to God on our behalf.

I had a relationship with God like no other, and I knew even back then that God and Jesus were my friends — closer and dearer to me than my mother, my grandmother, my pastor, or the missionaries could ever be. I remember having so much joy from knowing that I had God and Jesus as my friends, and I would start dancing in church and rejoicing. But I always had my eyes closed, and I'd be bumping into the pews and other people. Elder Chandler pulled me aside one day and said, "Open your eyes when you're praising God, son." Those words truly set me (and others) free.

When kids ask me today what the secret to my success is, I always say, "God. Put God first." I tell them, "Jesus will never fail you." And that I can say with certainty. God has never failed me. I have failed Him through my arrogance and with my ego. There was a time in my life when I dared to say there is no God, but still, Jesus kept me. I'm so thankful for my grandmother, mother, uncles, aunts, Elder Chandler, and all the missionaries, especially Missionary Taylor. I learned at an early age that I can do all things through Christ who strengthens me. Ironically, it was that supernatural faith that would later give me the courage to leave the church when they didn't agree with me going into acting. It was that supernatural faith that gave me the courage to excommunicate Elder Chandler and the church because I felt God had given me a direct order, and it actually scared me. But I knew I had to do it.

Nobody agreed with my decision to pursue my acting career, except my grandmother and one friend, Jake Smith. He was the only person who really believed that I'd become a great actor. I didn't meet Jake until I went to college. But it was Jake who really encouraged me to go into acting. He was the first one to tell me I was an actor, and that meant a lot to me.

It was my supernatural faith that revealed to me that no prophet, bishop, pope, or any other man had any authority over me. I knew I was a child of God, and there was no need to fear any man. That doesn't mean I don't respect those whom God has chosen to be leaders in his Church. What God settled in me, and what I want all of humanity to understand, is that God is the best bishop, prophet, missionary, evangelist, and teacher there ever was. Even with the great gifts that he has given us, we are all still human. I never felt I needed anyone's approval to know that I'm saved and that God loves me. And I feel sorry those who constantly seek God's validation through others. It's an insult to God. We're supposed to have a personal relationship with him. We can talk to God about anything. He loves us unconditionally, and he wants us to know it with certainty. We will never be able to comprehend the depth of God's love for us. When I think of how much he loves us, the song that says "the voices of a million angels cannot express my gratitude" comes to mind and expresses my heart. I am so grateful for his love, and the assurance it brings.

It hurt me to cut ties with Elder Chandler because I did love him. He was a father figure to me. From the age of twelve to eighteen, he was a positive male influence I could look up to.

Without the church, I felt alone. I began to vacillate between going back to the church and moving forward with my dreams. This was huge. Going against the theology of the very church I was once devoted to was one of the hardest decisions of my life.

I'll tell anyone, "Don't think that you're too young for God to speak to your soul." Look at David, who slew the giant Goliath as a young boy. God can speak to you directly and lead you to your purpose, ultimately enriching your life and, consequently, the lives of others. No church, religion, ideal, job, or person is more important that a relationship with God. He alone is the author of our faith. Having great relationships with family, friends, and spiritual leaders is important, but no one should be more important than him. He will never fail us. There are many uncertainties in this world, but faith in God gives us the ability to stand and move on. And that faith gave this scared, shy, skinny kid courage to exalt God above all the noise and distractions, above all the hate, all the uncertainty.

My grandmother was like Jesus walking this earth to me — she had such strong faith. But as a child, I was embarrassed whenever I went to church with her. I was embarrassed because she would start shouting like no one was there but her and Jesus. Her arms would be stretched out, thanking Jesus, crying and shouting. She loved Jesus so much that she didn't care what people thought. She was going to praise God no matter how she looked. And as I look back now, I really thank her for loving God more than anyone, giving no thought to others, me, or my embarrassment. Her faith strengthens me even today. Having faith and knowing God has been the foundation that has carried me all my life — even when I was in the devil's den, smoking a freebase pipe, flanked by orgies — is amazing. God still had me on his mind.

CHAPTER TWO

THE COLLEGE YEARS

Because I often played hooky in high school, I was a C+ student. So, in order to go to college, I had to take a summer course to prove I could handle college material. Ms. Thomas was instrumental in making that happen. I went to Indiana State University, in Terre Haute, Indiana, to study sociology and English.

It was the summer of 1967, and although I had experienced racism before, nothing prepared me for my encounter with my sociology professor, a man of Nazi German descent. He started the class off by saying, "I hate Jews, niggers, and miniskirts, in that order." Everyone just sat there in shock. He gave me a "B" on my final paper, and I was angry because I thought I should've gotten an "A." So, I went to his office to see him.

He had a decorated military uniform hanging on the back of the door. It was obvious he was a high-ranking officer. He had been drinking that day. I could smell the alcohol. I stated my case and told him I deserved an "A." His face turned blood red. He told me my paper was good, but not good enough to receive an "A." I told him I disagreed. Then I did an about-face and headed for the door. He said, "You know, the problem with you people is patience. You can't have equal rights overnight. Patience, damn it!" I really had to pray for restraint right then and there because I really wanted to choke the racial crap out of him that day.

Despite the racial divides and the often uneasy climate during that time, I met my first White friend that summer. His name was Steve. He looked like a young James Cagney, and he was very smart. I believe he got an "A" in the course, but he was White, so he wasn't on the "hate list." We often mocked our racist professor and did impersonations of him. Steve and I got along well, and I really thought we'd be buddies for life. But six weeks later, I was in his dorm room with some other students. And during that time, there was always something in the news about Dr. Martin Luther King leading nonviolent marches against racism and social injustice, and about the policemen who beat the protesters and Dr. King.

So, Steve and his White buddies began to tell me that Dr. King was out of order and that he was doing more harm than good. They felt he was hurting the Civil Rights Movement and was, instead, inciting riots. I did not agree with their position, nor did I like their comments at all. I was outnumbered, but I didn't care. I said right then and there: "This is over." I could never be friends with anyone who didn't respect Dr. King or his vision. I found their words to be insensitive to the fight for liberty and justice for all. And just like that, Steve was gone.

Friends do not and will not agree on everything, but some things cannot be overlooked. I did not want to associate with people who did not share in the dream for a better society. One thing I learned at an early age is that you have to watch the company you keep. And I thank God for giving me the ability to let people go. Bishop T. D. Jakes calls it "the gift of goodbye."

I'm one of the most loyal friends you can find — a true ride or die. I'll go through the fire for my friends. You'll never find a better friend than Ernest Thomas. However, some things are deal breakers. Betraying one's trust and disrespecting his or her beliefs, in my opinion, are grounds for separation. I cannot be best buddies with someone who does not believe in God and His Son — Jesus Christ. Some beliefs and principles are too dear, and when we refuse to take a stand for those beliefs and principles that we hold dear, we compromise who we really are for the gain of something or someone else. I could never do that. I had to stay true to who I was and what I believed.

I met my roommate, Greg Richey, during my freshman year. He was 6'3", and he was on the basketball team. We were total opposites. Greg cursed, and I didn't. He drank, and I didn't. He was having sex, and I wasn't. He looked at me like I was a freak because I didn't do any of those things.

Although Greg managed to study, he loved to party. He was a star basketball player, so he dated a lot of women. He mostly dated blonde White women, and at that time, that was dangerous in Terre Haute. The Ku Klux Klan marched every year in downtown Terre Haute.

But I admired Greg because he was a free spirit, and he didn't answer to anyone. He did whatever he wanted. He didn't take any mess from anybody. Any White guy who gave him a hard time about dating a White girl was punched in the mouth. After a few episodes, no one confronted him again. He didn't take any mess from Black guys either. A lot of them viewed him as a sell-out or a traitor because he dated only White girls. But Greg wasn't prejudiced by any means. If you respected him, he respected you.

I never told him that I admired the freedom he had, but I did. He was truly a free spirit. Greg also loved to pull pranks. Because I was a skinny, little, naïve, and scared church boy who was afraid of my own shadow, he would often hide in the closet. And when I least expected it, which was usually when I was returning from studying at the local diner, he would jump out of the closet, screaming at the top of his lungs. I would jump out of my skin every time. It never failed.

One night, after Greg came back to the room drunk after a night of partying, I reprimanded him about his lifestyle and started telling him about the Gospel of Jesus Christ and his need to get saved. Greg kindly told me to mind my own business. He said, "You do you, and I'll do me," and we did. We still remained good friends because he was a good guy. We simply agreed to disagree.

During freshman year, we had freshman initiation, where the upper classmen would haze the freshman. They would throw them in the shower with their clothes on, put shaving cream in their underwear, blindfold them and have them reach inside the toilet for what they thought was something else, but was actually a banana, and many other outlandish acts. So, I decided I would avoid that night. I stayed out until two a.m., figuring everyone would be asleep by then. I slowly opened the door to my dorm room, taking my clothes off and feeling relieved. I had gotten away with it, or so I thought. But, just as

I was about to get in the bed, Greg jumped out of bed, opened the door, and yelled, "He's here now!" All the freshmen and upper classmen doused me with buckets of water. I got the full-throttle hazing, while Greg pointed his finger in my face and doubled over in laughter.

Later on in the semester, Greg decided to go into the movie business. He began showing movies in our dorm room and charging 25 cents for admission. These were mature movies, so the showings were late at night and on the weekends. In addition to watching Greg's movies, I started hanging out late, just having a great time with the fellas, telling jokes, listening to music, watching television, and going to the Pancake House. There were a couple of guys on our floor who were very funny, and we had lots of fun telling jokes. But no studying, along with creating comedy, listening to music, and watching movies, was a good recipe for failure. I had a 1.7 grade point average during my first semester. It was quite alarming! But God blessed me with a friend, Rick Nichols, who would help me get back on the right track. I thank God for Rick, and we are still friends today. Rick was an "A" student, and he kept to himself most of the time. He was a sophomore, and he was friendly. But he came to class to learn, not to socialize. For some reason, he liked me, and we became friends. I was the envy of everyone. He said, "I know your mother and your grandmother did not send you here to party. If you wanna study, and you're serious, we can study together. But only if you're serious." Rick was a White guy with a black belt in karate. After studying, we'd sometimes catch a movie, and Rick would say: "I wish someone would call you the "N" word!"

We would go to the movies, and Rick would be waiting for someone to say something, but no one ever did. Rick was truly one in a million. During our study breaks, we would talk about our families, racism, the Church, and what I experienced as a kid growing up in Gary without a father. He had a father. I asked him if his mother and father ever thought negatively about black people. He said, "Never." He took me to meet them. It was truly a wonderful experience. I believe they had to be the friendliest people in Albany, Indiana. That was the first time I had been in a mostly White town. But they made me feel right at home. Rick's father, Charles, was very funny. He always wore a smile and laughed often. Rick's mother was a beautiful brunette who was an amazing cook. His sister was a few years younger than he was, but they were very close. It was just like being with family, and I received their love.

Shortly after my visit, Rick came to Gary, Indiana, which was predominantly Black, and stayed with me, my mother, grandmother, sister, and brother for the weekend. And they fell in love with Rick. Mom made a ham for him, and I'm almost certain he ate the whole ham! He ate a lot.

Rick was my first White friend, but I had a few others — Artie Zuckerman, Paul Goldstein, Jay Schechter, and Finkelstein. We had a lot of laughs together, and they understood the struggle. But that's because they were Jewish. I didn't know that much about Jewish people back then. Finkelstein reminded me of a thin version of myself because he wore the "Raj" black glasses. Artie and I became very close friends, like brothers. He took me to his home in New York, and I met his mother, father, aunts, and uncles. They had the best food, and they told jokes all the time. They were so quick with the come-backs. They talked about how much they admired Dr. King and about what their relatives went through during the holocaust. The horrific history and anti-Semitism that they suffered unit-ed them as a family. Artie once said, "When my uncle became successful with his business, he helped my father and then they helped another relative. This is what Blacks should do." I agreed with him.

One day Paul came to my dorm room and said he need-ed to talk to me. He came in and broke down in tears. He had just discovered that he had some prejudice in him, and he was shocked and scared by it. His girlfriend had just told him that she had had a black boyfriend before she'd met him. That made him extremely angry, so enraged that he slapped her. He then realized that he wasn't as liberal as he thought. I said, "But you're still a good guy. At least you're not proud of it. You admitted it and came to me about it. You're a standup guy." I really appreciated Paul's honesty and respected him for dis-cussing the incident and how he felt about it with me.

I think we all have some prejudice in us. If not about color, it could be about weight or height or the way a person dresses or a person's religion or any number of things. We're hopeful it's not against a race. But, as President Clinton once said, "We fear each other because we don't know each other." We tend to shun those we do not identify with, making it easy for us to create walls of separation and indifference. And I think that's what we have to pray that God chips away at every day.

Jay was probably the one White Jewish student that car-ried the struggle for equal and civil rights on his shoulders. He loved everything black. He wanted to be Black, and he always talked about Black people being the first people God created — that Adam and Jesus were Black, and all the prophets were Black. He would go to McDonald's and pay for all the Black students' food. He loved his Jewish heritage and Jewish people, but he thought Blacks had it rougher because we could never hide our blackness. He was sincere. I felt sorry for him because he was truly frustrated because he wasn't Black.

I became a Kappa man during my sophomore year. Greg had told me that Arthur Ash and Ralph Bunche were members, and I was ready to pledge. However, my one regret about my college experience is that I didn't go to church at all. I didn't even realize it at the time. I still believed in God, but I just didn't go to church. And when I started to pledge, I started to drink, and I learned how to use profanity. I hated drinking. My fellow pledging brothers would say, "Keep drinking. You'll acquire a taste for it." They were right. I started drinking all the time. Soon, I looked forward to drinking cold beer every day. We didn't drink every day, but we drank at least a couple of times a week. I loved pledging. The only time I was on the honor roll was during the time I was pledging, and one of the happiest days of my life was when I became a member of Kappa Alpha Psi. Our line was called "17 Spartans," and all my brothers were like real brothers, like blood brothers to me, especially Ivory Smith. He was my best friend. I had several friends, but I considered Ivory, Rick, and Jake to be my closest friends at that time. Jake was Ivory's brother, and he was two years older than I was. He had been in the Army, and he knew a lot. God placed him in my life to be that big brother I needed. He was a strong brother, and he was fascinated with my imitations of people on television. He thought I was hilarious. And that's how it all started. None of this fame would be possible if God hadn't put it on Jake's heart.

One time I was performing and trying to make him laugh, and he said these prophetic words: "You're an actor, and you can do whatever those actors are doing on television and in the movies." He really stunned me. I said, "What are you talking about? I'm just being silly. I'm going to be a social worker." He said, "Just take a course and see what happens." So I did.

I took Acting 101 after seeing *Romeo and Juliet* in the theaters. Franco Zeffirelli had done a beautiful retelling of the Romeo and Juliet story. It was enchanting, seductive, poignant, tragic, and funny. I saw it many times. I loved the costumes, the language, the poetry: "A rose by any other name would smell as sweet." Shakespeare's work is just amazing.

I fell in love with Acting 101 immediately. The class was filled with students majoring in theater. I just went on what I felt instinctively. For the final exam, I had to do three monologues. So, I did Julius Caesar's "To Be Or Not To Be," from *Hamlet*, Prince Scalas (his speech in *Romeo and Juliet*), and Abraham Lincoln's *Gettysburg Address*. I had taken the sheets off my bed and wrapped them around me. The class was amused by my appearance. But when I started talking and I had their attention, something very scary started to happen. I felt at home on that stage. I felt empowered by the character. I felt high. *"What is going on?"* I thought to myself. And the professor said, "You can do this for a living, you know?" I said, "Oh, no. I want to be a social worker. But thank you." God works in many ways and through many things. I was the least likely to become an actor in that class. I had no acting experience. I had no intentions of pursuing something that I felt was foreign to me except when I was on stage.

One of the things I liked most about my college years was the unity and togetherness of the Black students on campus. I loved the camaraderie. And, in spite of the division and often volatile racial climate in the country during that time, one could meet people from all walks of life and many different countries right there on campus. I had a great deal of fun in college. And I loved that I was fighting for the civil rights of my people. Despite the hateful and violent acts that we saw televised daily, people of all races and creeds marched together peacefully for the rights of those who were oppressed. I couldn't understand how White Christians who said they believed in Jesus Christ could hate their fellow Black sisters and brothers in Christ. Dr. King once said Sunday is the most segregated and divided day of the week. Back then, a Black Christian could have been killed for stepping into a White church in the South.

My mother is eighty-six years old, and she was raised in Mississippi. She was angry about racism and the injustices she and others experienced, but she loves God too much to hate anyone. I look at my mother in awe because I wonder how she could keep her sanity after all the things she witnessed in Mississippi as a child. I know her faith in God and his love is what kept her strong and helped her survive those experiences.

Although I believe pledging Kappa was and is a blessing, I also believe I failed God. I should have joined the fraternity without losing my relationship with him. The Kappas didn't put a gun to my head and force me to drink. I wanted to fit in. But, what if I had just said, "I'm not drinking. I don't like alcohol. I'm not going to use profanity, and I'll still be one of the best in history"? Don't get me wrong; all my brothers believed in God, but they loved to party and enjoy life, too. Truth be told, I just wanted to party, too. I was tired of being a boring goody two shoes. We were young, and we were supposed to enjoy life, but the key to success in life is to have the proper balance. Having a relationship with God keeps us in the right place and helps us to experience far less heartache and pain. The Bible tells us not to lean on our own understanding. Keeping God first and talking to him daily gives us the wisdom we need, and I believe if I had kept communicating with him during that time I would have been a better person for it. I often say God loved me so much He allowed me to play hooky.

Being a Kappa man made me feel seven feet tall—proud, confident, and sure. Pledging was a training in manhood for me. I grew up in a house full of women, and I know for a fact I was a bit feminine. My uncles were strong, masculine men, but I wasn't around them often. Being around these confident brothers during my college years gave me an extra backbone. I credit Ivory for being my main role model. I tried to emulate the way he walked and talked. I tried to imitate his coolness. All my frat brothers were powerful, strong, Black men. I followed their example and became a strong, Black man in the process. God surely uses many things to work for our good.

Amazingly, my first acting gig was as Prince Escalus in *Romeo and Juliet*. God is awesome. I was in denial with this acting thing, but I had fallen in love with Shakespeare. In Franco

Zeffirelli's adaptation, Prince Escalus was played by the great Robert Stephens. He was supernatural. You gotta see it! He had this commanding presence, and his voice was from another world. When I had my audition, I imitated him. I jumped on stage and did my best impression of Robert Stephens' version of Prince Escalus, and as I was about to walk off the stage, the director said, "I don't know about you guys, but I want to hear that one more time." It was amazing. I got the role and a vote of confidence from the director as well.

We traveled to schools throughout Indiana, and I signed my first autograph on the university program. I loved everything about theater. I loved being around a positive group of actors who supported one another. We had lots of fun. One night Romeo mixed up a line, and everyone in the scene was about to lose it. Our bodies were trembling with laughter. I had to turn away from the audience and hold my breath to keep from laughing out loud. But then we all let it out. We couldn't keep it together any longer. The audience knew Romeo had mixed up a line, and it was hilarious. So the audience laughed with us. But our stage manger wasn't pleased at all.

In one city, while we were on stage, the Black actor who played the role of Mercutio was in the middle of one his lines when someone yelled out the "N" word. The actor kept going. We all kept going. The audience gave us a standing ovation. And what made the day even better was when the White boy who had said "nigger" came to us and apologized.

After the tour was over, I decided to focus on my studies and forget acting. But it was not long after making that decision that I felt a void inside me. I felt out of place, and I longed to be on stage. I felt like I was floating, and going nowhere.

On April 4, 1968, Dr. King died. After hearing the "Mountain Top" speech and knowing he had been murdered, it was devastating. I couldn't move. Even now, whenever I hear that speech, I start crying. I love that speech.

Who could do something so evil to such a great man? Black people in Terre Haute and all over America were furious, and started riots. Dr. King would have been so disappointed about the rioting. But people were enraged because a man who stood for peace was murdered.

I was angry, too. So many emotions were felt that day. I was in the lobby of my dorm when the elevator doors opened and some White kids came off the elevator with guns and hunting rifles, chanting "Kill the niggers, kill the niggers." These were the same White guys I had seen every day. So, the police had to protect the Black students from the White students. Most White students weren't participating in the attacks, but there were certainly enough, even some of the cops to part in the attacks. It was a very trying time.

Shortly after that, as a member of the Young Democrats, I remember meeting Robert Kennedy. He was at a parade. He saw me, and he reached out to grab my hand. He looked exhausted. He was assassinated a short time later, and his brother, President John Kennedy had been assassinated just five years earlier. I remember thinking that if these men were being murdered, what would happen to me, and others like me? I felt like the only thing I could do was pray.

I was given a voice through the Black Student Union. They wanted me to start a column in the main student newspaper so we could be heard. The column was called Pamoja , which, in Swahili, means together. We even had peaceful demonstrations in the administration building from time to time.

In one of my articles for the column, I attacked the credibility of the white professor who was in charge of creating a Black history program at the university. He was just a figure head — incompetent, with no strategy, compassion, or vision about how to create such a program. After the article was published, all hell broke loose. The professor was going to sue the paper and the university for defamation of character. I was asked to recant and apologize, but I refused. Even the president of the university asked me to apologize. When I refused, he even asked a Black professor of sociology to talk to me. I met with him and kindly thanked him for meeting with me. But I knew I was right, and I was prepared to stand up for what I believed in.

Shortly after, the Black history professor resigned and dropped his lawsuit. The university hired a Jewish female professor as his replacement. She was awesome, and she obviously appreciated the achievements of Black people. Many signed up, and it was a huge class, with an equal number of White and Black students. It turned out to be a wonderful and enlightening experience.

Then there was the Vietnam War. I had to get a physical to see if I qualified for the draft. I considered myself a conscientious objector. I don't believe any of us would object to fighting if it was for a just cause or for our families. But no one understood the war and why we were in it. I admired Muhammad Ali for not going. Because of his stand, he was suspended from boxing during his prime, right after winning the heavyweight title. He was willing to die. That empowered me. I had never heard a Black man speak like he did, especially with so much to lose and the threat of five years in prison. I admired him long before I even met him. He educated America on racism. He asked, "Why is everything white considered pure and everything black considered evil? A white cake is called 'angel food cake,' but a black cake is called 'devil's food cake.'" He taught America that "Black is beautiful."

The night before my physical, I purposely got drunk. Jake offered to drive me, but I was confident that I could drive. After breaking up with my first car, the "pink whale," I found a good deal on a white Pontiac that had been formerly owned by an elderly couple. It had only a few miles on it and was in good shape. So I hopped in the Pontiac and headed for Indianapolis to take my physical. I had been up all night, so when I got in the car, I rolled the windows down so I could feel the cool morning air and stay awake. There I was driving with the wind in my face. All of a sudden—yes, you guessed it. I fell asleep at the wheel. I heard this bump, bump, bump. It was the car hitting mailboxes. When I woke up, I frantically tried to avoid the oncoming traffic and ended up at the door of this White lady's house. She came out and said, "Are you alright?" All I could do was nod, because my head was in a fog. She said, "Well, OK—as long as you're alright. I have to work." I was shocked by her reaction. She wasn't angry, and she didn't call the police. She had Christ in her for sure. Now, the other people across the street with the leaning mailboxes didn't look too happy, but I knew I had to face the music. I started acting immediately. I put on that face that always helped me get my way with my mother, grandmother, friends, and even strangers — that face that no one wanted to say no to. I gave them the face and let them talk. The men were angry, but the women saw that face and shut the men down. They asked, "Where are you going?" I said, "To take my physical for the draft. My mother is worried to death because I am her only son." One of the ladies, whom everybody seemed to respect, took over the conversation. She said "I can understand why your mother would be worried. My son is in Vietnam." They didn't call the police. Instead, they bid me farewell with the physical and gave me their blessings, even the men. I went to take the physical, but I didn't pass. I was legally blind in one eye. Who knew? I did not know. But let me be clear; I have great respect for soldiers who go out to war so we can have our freedom at home. But I was relieved that I didn't have to fight in a war that I didn't understand.

I would love to say that was the only time I fell asleep at the wheel, but I can't. A few months later, I fell asleep on the way back to Terre Haute from Gary. I hit an elderly White couple in their van. They were so sweet. I couldn't believe God's grace. They had every reason to be upset, but they weren't. The police came, and I got a ticket for driving without a license and car insurance. Now, here's an example of the favor of God. Later on I went to court for my tickets. I was waiting for my case to be called. There were a few cases ahead of mine. When my name was called, I got up to go stand before the judge, and all of a sudden, the power in city went out. The judge dismissed the rest of the cases and told everyone to go home. Hello, some-body! God is real!

But there was a time when I did question the existence of God. It started in my philosophy class. The professor was an atheist, and he took advantage of every chance he got to share his atheist beliefs. He would say things with fake kind-ness, claiming he was trying to steer us on the right path in life. I don't remember when I started buying into it, but by the time the course was over, I had become a bonafide atheist.

I went to the frat house and shared my new revelation: there was no God. The frat brothers — the ones who had women on the side, cussed, drank, and partied — all lit into me. "Oh, there is a God!" they said. We argued for hours. I left that night feeling very conflicted. Before I went to bed, I asked God: "Are you real? Forgive me for asking." I can't say God spoke to me. God is a spirit. But he spoke to me in my spirit, and I felt his presence. I was soon back on track with God. I was still drink-ing and cussing, and not going to church. But I believed!

It was customary to try to have as many one-night stands as possible as a Kappa. And women love Kappa men — mar-ried, single, Black, White, and all in-between. My brothers were very popular with the women. But I can count on one hand the women I've gone to bed with. This has a lot to do with my religious upbringing, but it also is due to being naturally shy. I'm still not comfortable with strangers. I will never understand how a man can go to a bar, meet a total stranger, and then take her some place and have sex with her. It is beyond my com-prehension. However, if drinking is involved, then it is easier to understand. Drinking gave me courage to be like my frat brothers. I really wanted to impress them, so I brought a college girl to the frat house so I could impress them. This girl and I had known each other since grade school. And I always knew she had a crush on me, but we were just friends. So I bought a six-pack of Schlitz Malt Liquor. My frat brother said that it got women in the mood and made it easier for them to give in.

I'm not proud of this moment, but I want to be open and transparent about my experiences. I took her to one of the bedrooms in the frat house. She was an old-fashioned girl, so she trusted me. I chose her because I couldn't have sex with a stranger. I came out of the bedroom in my underwear like I was a conqueror, and all my brothers were smiling. They were so proud of me, giving me high-fives. "It's about time," they said. I never invited a girl to the house again after that.

The girl's sister was upset because I had made her sister nothing more than a booty call, and she told me I needed to apologize or else. I must admit, I was scared. She looked very athletic, like she had kicked a man's butt before. She had a de-termined look in her eyes as she came nose to nose with me. I was acting tough to save face in front of my frat brothers. They jumped between us, but she continued to talk about what I needed to do and what she would do to me. She was justified in her actions. I would've done the same thing. I was so ashamed and depressed because I couldn't apologize. I felt the brothers would think I was weak, but the God in me wanted to apolo-gize and ask the girl and her sister for their forgiveness.

I didn't apologize for years, but it always haunted me. I think I was a student in acting school when I called her to apol-ogize. I told her I was sorry for what I had done and that I was trying to impress my frat brothers. I told her that what I had done to her was despicable. She started crying because she didn't expect me to admit that to her after so many years had passed. Years later, I ran into a friend of hers who told me she had died a few years before, and she had told her friend how much it had meant to her that I had asked for her forgiveness. That gave me tremendous joy and peace. But from time to time, I still look back with regret on how I hurt her.

I'm not proud of all the choices I've made. But, who is? Yet we have to forgive ourselves and choose to learn from the mistakes and bad decisions we make, choosing to make better decisions going forward. Thankfully, I've done considerably more good than bad in this world. Staying true to my beliefs and my character has helped me to avoid many pitfalls and shortcomings in my life. We can never be perfect. There was only One who was, in this earth. But we can choose to give the best representation of ourselves to the world, choosing love over hate, giving over taking, healing over killing, unity over separation. This life is truly a gift from God, and it's up to us to make the most of it, and hopefully that means making it a better place than it was without us.

CHAPTER THREE

NEW YORK, NEW YORK

I was just going through the motions in graduate school because the acting bug was still haunting me. It was like an itch that kept coming back. I tried to shake it, but to no avail. It was so insane, the thought of me pursuing acting as a career. It sounds insane even now. It sounds insane every time I think about it. I was a loner, incredibly shy. Yes, I would do characters and make Jake laugh, but I was basically a nerd. I'm the least likely type of person to become an actor. I often think about all those students I met who were majoring in theater. Those students were passionate, and theater was their life. They spent four years perfecting their crafts. I could under-stand why they laughed at me as I walked on that stage with authority in Acting 101. I spoke with authority, as if I had been doing it for years. With their limited vision, they couldn't see what God saw. I couldn't see it either. And that's why it's so important to keep feelings in their proper place and in the proper lane.

Feelings are traitors to the soul, traitors to the goal, traitors to the dream, traitors to freedom and happiness. Even as I write this autobiography, I'm amazed that God had a purpose for me that was far greater than I could have ever imagined. But I had to override the array of feelings — doubt, fear, self-pity, low self-esteem, and unworthiness — that overwhelmed me at times. Whenever those emotions try to take a hold of me, I run to the secret place of the most high that David spoke about in Psalm 91.

We need the crucifixion of all those negative feelings and the resurrection of our supernatural being on a daily basis. As children of the most high God, we don't have to apologize for being gifted or great. God never apologized or was shy about being the Creator of everything in the heavens and on the earth. Jesus never backed down from what he was here on this earth to do. Once we grasp this knowledge and meditate on it, we can ask anything that is in line with his plans for us, in Jesus' name, and He will do it. With God, all things are possible to those who believe.

I received my degree in sociology and psychology, and I was proud of that achievement. I was grateful to God for such a huge blessing, not realizing that God had so much more for me than I could imagine in my wildest dreams. All I had to do was obey the voice of God and dismiss all the doubters and haters among my family and friends.

I was in a constant state of vulnerability, not quite sure what the future held for me. But I knew God was with me, and he would lead me to my destiny. Initially, I looked to the goal that was attainable: becoming a social worker. In graduate school, my goal was to become a dean at a university. But God used Jake to remind me of the greatness that was ahead of me. I wasn't happy in grad school. I was assistant dorm director at the time, and even with all its perks, I was not happy. Yet I dared not say what my heart yearned for: to be an actor. The thought of it scared me but overwhelmed me so much that I would whisper it to myself when I was alone. I'd ask God, "What's going on with me?" I couldn't tell anyone that I was even thinking about it. Jake was the only one who knew because God had spoken it into Jake's heart, and he had spoken it into mine.

But I had responsibilities. I was the first one in my family to graduate from college. They were expecting me to get a great job and be successful so I could help the family financially. That was something I'd been wanting to do all my life. Going to college, being successful, and having a good job, great money, and a nice home had always been my dream. I'd been told all my life, by my uncles, my aunts, our neighbors, my teachers, and my pastor, that I was the one. "Ernie is going to be something great. He's definitely going to college. He's definitely going to graduate from college," they'd say.

Everything had been going smoothly in that direction until Jake put a monkey wrench in what seemed to be the perfect plan, and I couldn't shake it off. I couldn't shake my love for acting. When you're in love, you do everything you can to please the object of your affection. I wanted to please her, but I didn't know how, and I didn't want to admit that I was in love with her. Thinking about acting and reflecting on the little I had achieved in the play and in class bathed me in waves of euphoria I never thought possible, and I didn't want it to end. I craved more of it in my mind and in my heart. But my family and everyone else was expecting me to have a regular nine-to-five job and be happy. I'm not knocking anyone who works a nine-to-five job, it just wasn't my calling.

Everyone must take a leap of faith that seems scary and impossible, but once taken, it will lead to something great. Most people run from it to stay in their comfort zones and be content with remaining where they are. And that's what happened to me. Logic and reason said get your degree, get a job, please your family and friends, and shut up about your real dream. Logic said, "It's ridiculous to think you can make a living as an actor when so many talented actors don't work most of the time. Statistically, it's totally insane to go into acting as a career." Reason said, "You have very little experience to compare with all those actors with degrees in acting and with acting experience. Many of them have been acting since they were kids." Logic said, "Ernest Thomas, stay in your lane or you're going to make a fool of yourself." Reason said, "Your mother and grandmother will be disappointed in you." The devil said, "All the folks that love you will hate you if you pursue this dumb idea of becoming an actor."

But the God in me kept nudging me to go against the fear and go into the unknown and the uncomfortable. I was asking God, "How am I going to do it? How, Lord? Show me the way. I don't know." All the while, I was attending my classes and focusing on becoming a dean.

I did take a test for a social worker position, but I had failed it. I believe I subconsciously did it on purpose. After I failed the test, that's when I had decided to go to graduate school to study student personnel. And I honestly thought I was excited about attending grad school and becoming a dean, but I was in denial. I was just going through the motions.

Meanwhile, Jake told me he had seen an ad in the *Chicago Tribune* about the American Academy of Dramatic Arts, in New York, one of the top schools in the world for actors. The school was holding auditions in Chicago for its fall classes. Their graduates are some of the best in entertainment: Robert Redford, Spencer Tracy, Lauren Bacall, and Cecil DeMille, just to name a few. It is the oldest English-speaking acting school in the world. Jake was so excited when he brought me the newspaper, but when I looked at the long list of great actors, I said to myself, *"Jake is out of his mind!"* And then I said, "Jake, do you see all these stars who attended this school? The Academy doesn't want me." Jake said, "We're going to this audition. I saw the list, and you're going to get accepted. You can do anything they can do." Jake was making me angry. I didn't want to go. Then he said, "If you don't go, I'll kick your ass!" If I had been a little bigger at the time and knew some martial arts, I think I could've taken Jake. But nobody messed with Jake, nobody. After a little more encouragement from Jake, I finally agreed to go to the audition.

Jake drove me to Chicago. I decided I was going to do the Prince Escalus speech from *Romeo and Juliet* and then tie in several passages from *Death of a Salesman* and make that my monologue. I knew the Prince Escalus monologue would be very dramatic and loud, but the *Death of Salesman* monologue would be more poignant, introspective, and intimate. So I had a nice contrast, which would give me the opportunity to show my versatility and range.

Chicago is about 200 miles from Terre Haute, so Jake really had to believe in me to travel that far. When we arrived and parked in front of the LaSalle Hotel, I felt sudden waves of fear and rejection. I didn't know what to believe anymore, but I knew for sure that I didn't want to go to that audition. I felt I wasn't good enough, but I didn't want to fight Jake. I just knew I was going to humiliate myself, but Jake's certainty was amazing. I never saw an ounce of doubt in him at all. There were moments when his confidence angered me. But looking back now, I know he was a blessing from God. No matter what I said, he wasn't budging, and he was willing to kick my butt and make me audition if he had to. In fact, he was so certain I was going to get accepted that he bought a six-pack of Schlitz Malt Liquor to celebrate. I knew it was time to man up.

I went in asking God for strength to have a successful audition. Charles Raison, the executive director of the Academy, greeted me. He had a kind demeanor, with a commanding and professional presence. But he made me feel welcome and comfortable. He told me to start whenever I was ready. So I grabbed one of the hotel chairs in his suite, jumped on top of it, and delivered the Prince Escalus speech. Then I sat in the chair and did the *Death of a Salesman* monologue. After I was done, he extended his hand with a smile and said, "Welcome to the American Academy of Dramatic Arts." I almost fainted. He cautioned me to be careful not to become my own audience when performing. As he spoke, I stood there looking at him as if he were a ghost, thinking: *"What did you say?"* I thanked him and then he gave me literature and pamphlets about the Academy. I was officially in the supernatural zone, meaning I knew that God's hand was on my life, which was exciting and scary at the same time. I knew on that very day that my life would never be the same, and I would have to withstand the tsunami of opposition from my family, church, friends, and frat brothers. But I didn't care because everything around me let me know that God was in the midst of it all.

Something that I had thought was essentially impossible had now become a reality. I couldn't get to Jake's car fast enough. "He said ,'Welcome to the American Academy of Dramatic Arts'!" I said to Jake as soon as I got in the car. Jake said, "What did I tell you? Let's drink!" Man, that cold Schlitz Malt Liquor never tasted better. I sat there thinking, *"God, now what? Lord, I was accepted. Now I gotta get some money."* I was also thinking about Jake. I didn't stare at him, but I wanted to — not in lust, but out of sheer admiration. I glanced at him and asked God within myself, *"Who is he? God, you sent this man who has seven other siblings and a beautiful fiancée. And here he is taking time out for me as if I were his blood brother."* He definitely didn't have to spend his time nurturing me and stirring supernatural faith in me to believe that I could be an actor, but he did.

I asked Jake years later why he felt so strongly about my gift as an actor and why he spent so much time with me. He said it made him happy. When I got the role of Roger Thomas on *What's Happening!!*, Jake refused to take one dime from me. I even offered him ten percent to be my manager. He said his reward was the joy that came from seeing me on the screen. He was a godsend. God truly does bless us through friendships.

Having someone in your corner who believes in you whole-heartedly and cares about you enough to help you take those leaps of faith when you're afraid to jump should be valued and treasured. These are the gems God gives us to help us reach all that he has in store for us in this life.

Thanks to Jake, I was now in this supernatural zone, and I couldn't tell anyone. What was I going to say to Mom and my family, friends, and frat brothers? I decided to shut up and wait.

There was a job opening in Portage, Indiana, at Midwest Steel Mill. Portage was a predominantly White city, and most of the workers at the steel mill were White. Affirmative action was a big deal at that time. It was especially important in all-White industries or companies. I applied for the assistant human relations director position, and I got it. I would be assisting the human relations director, an older White guy who was very flamboyant and liked to wear loud ties and expensive suits. He'd been in that position for several decades, and they were planning to groom me to take his position once he retired. I wasn't interested in a long-term position or assuming his role. My eyes were on the Academy and saving enough money for tuition in the fall. In addition to putting money away for the Academy, I also helped Mom and Grandma with some extra money, and I often gave my brother and sister money, too. It made me feel good to know I was helping, and it also helped ease the guilt I felt about the upcoming announcement I would soon have to make about attending the Academy.

While working at Midwest Steel Mill, I became close friends with one of the secretaries there. Her name was Sandy, but she looked like a young Carol Burnett. She managed a rock band on the side, and it was fun being with her because she was cute, and she managed a rock band, which I thought was hot. We flirted with each other a lot. I had an office in the back of the building, away from everyone else. So, she would often stop by. We would have lunch, and then make out. We didn't have sex, but we came pretty close to it. It was exciting getting away with it. Then, all of a sudden, I was being summoned into my supervisor's office. He was a semi-stocky guy with black hair and glasses, and he smoked a pipe. Although he was young, he dressed conservatively, like an older man. The head supervisor was a thin man with blondish hair, and he also wore glasses. I thought I was there for a review of my job performance, but when I got in the office, they informed me that I had been accused of sexual harassment. I had no words. I felt betrayed. They said Sandy had filed a complaint against me. I felt like I had been hit in the gut by Mike Tyson! It really knocked the wind out of me. Me? Sexual harassment? They were only going on what she had told them, and because she had been there much longer than I had, it seemed they believed her. They were enjoying the fact that they had something on me. They said, "Well, we're going to reprimand you with a warning this time." They went on about Sandy being a good employee, and they knew her character and her work ethic. I was livid! But I returned to my office, reminding myself that I'd be leaving in a few months to go to the Academy. I wanted to curse them all out, but I remembered what my mother always says: "Ease your hand out of the lion's mouth." And I recalled the scripture that says "Life and death lies in the tongue." So, I knew I had to keep quiet. I needed that income for acting school, and to help support my family.

After that meeting, I would give Sandy polite "good mornings," but nothing else. I knew she was poison. They may have gotten a good laugh at my expense, but I knew God was on my side. Go ahead. Talk behind my back. You got me today. But I will win tomorrow. Trust me.

When my six months were up, I couldn't wait to hand in my resignation letter. I wish I had brought in a camera to catch their reactions. BAM! I was outta there! Months later, Sandy sent an apology letter to me at the Academy. She said I had inspired her to pursue her dreams in music. And, of course, I forgave her. I had already won. The best revenge is success.

After resigning, I was excited about going to the Academy, but I had to finally tell my mother, grandmother, and friends that I was going to school to become an actor, and that I had resigned from my position at the steel mill. It didn't go over too well. My folks don't yell, and they don't use guilt. But it didn't feel good to be told by everyone that I was making a mistake. My grandmother didn't mind. She saw how happy acting made me. My mother and my friends kept reminding that I was leaving a good job with a steady income to go to acting school in New York and start all over again after already earning a college degree.

I was not very popular with the home crowd, which was hard for me because I loved being liked by everyone in my circle. But I've come to learn that I may not always be popular with family, friends, or even cliques, but I am enough. With Christ, we are always enough. Know that you and Christ are the majority. With him on your side, there is nothing you cannot do.

I had enough money for my tuition, but I didn't have enough for an apartment. A friend told me that his sister-in-law would let me live with her and her family. I was told I didn't have to pay rent. I only had to help out with buying groceries when I got a job.

When I arrived in New York, my friend's sister-in-law and her husband picked me up at the airport. When we got home, she prepared a great dinner, and I enjoyed getting to know the family. Later that night, after everyone had gone to bed, my friend's sister-in-law came in my room to talk to me, among other things. She told me that my rent would be free if I took care of her sexual needs on the side. I was shocked. I told her I was flattered, but I could never do what she was suggesting. She said, "Oh, no problem." The following morning, during breakfast, she told me I would have to move because she had relatives coming from out of town to live with them, and they would be needing what I had thought was my room. That was the end of that.

I called the Academy and was told that they had an agreement with the Roger Williams Hotel, where three students could live in a room for 100 dollars each, per month. I got a job at the Academy helping out in the office. The job didn't pay much, but it did help.

My roommates were Marty Robinson and Jim Kott, an Irish kid who was an arts major at Pratt Institute. Marty and Jim were great roommates, and we got along well. Jim was a free spirit and was proud of his Irish roots. He would treat me to a few beers on the weekend at this Irish pub. He knew I didn't have a lot of extra money, so he always wanted to treat me to dinner. We had lots of fun together. When I got the part in *What's Happening!!*, he called me and said, "Ernie, don't you owe me something?" I was a little upset because I didn't think he should have asked me that way. So I said, "No, I don't owe you anything." He said, "No? You don't owe me anything?" I said, "No."

I chose to write this book for several reasons. I want to thank people I took for granted, and make amends for mistakes I've made. But most importantly, I want to acknowledge and celebrate how God helped me overcome and succeed through faith. So, Jim Kott, if you read this, I apologize from the bottom of my heart. And, yes, I do owe you, a lot.

The American Academy of Dramatic Arts provided a competitive two-year program to 200 students. At the end of the program, sixty of the students are chosen. I wanted to be in that number. My first teacher was Betsy Chevy, a pretty Jewish lady. She said, "Acting is: 'what do I want from each character, and what am I going to do to get it?'"

Occasionally, the Academy would have special guests stop by to talk to us and give us wisdom and insight. One particular time they didn't tell us who the guest was going to be. Then Robert Redford stepped out on the stage. He needed no introduction. We were actually screaming with excitement. He spoke for about two hours. He told us to "be bad big!" In other words, try things outside your comfort zone so you can possibly stumble on magic. He mentioned happy mistakes — not doing things the same way. Discovery. Being open to accidents

and mistakes. He captivated us for two whole hours and answered all our questions. He was amazing. I'm sure none of us
has forgotten that day.

At the end of our first year at the Academy, the staff cast
us in several plays to determine if we'd be selected to return
for the second year. I was cast as the Ragpicker in *Madwoman
of Chaillot*. Another gifted student named Andrew was also
cast in that role. We were never allowed to see the other actors' performances. You had to focus on your own take on the
characters and give it the "supernatural stank" God gave you.
Supernatural stank is that intangible magic that is uniquely
yours, given only by God. Most people run away from it, because in order to reach it you have to "BE BAD BIG" and be
willing to think outside the box.

My director made me do just that. He knew that Andrew,
a classically trained actor, would do it the traditional way. He
asked, "What can you do different?" I hadn't thought about
it. I had planned to go the traditional route as well. So the director suggested doing the scene as a hip street guy. That was
definitely out of my comfort zone because I wasn't hip or street-
wise. But I thought about all my frat brothers, and certain ones,
in particular, came to mind that I could pull from. I had no idea
what I did, but I know I felt totally high, and I didn't want to
stop. Once we ignited the hip street guy, I was all in. At one
point, I think I grabbed my crotch and was about to pull my
pants down. The director said, "Ernest, there's a line. But it's
great that you're willing to go all the way. It's better to be too
much than to be boring." I never wanted to be boring.

I was ecstatic about being selected for the second year of classes. Andrew wasn't called back, but I really believe he was more talented. He could do Shakespeare, and he knew a lot about theater. He talked about it all the time. There were other people who didn't get selected who I thought were more talented. However, when you resurrect the SUPERNATURAL STANK all eyes are on you, no matter who's on stage. It's divine, it's other worldly. It can't be taught. It's a faith thing, a belief thing.

During our second year at the Academy, we did more plays. The Academy invited directors and producers to attend. I was in a short play written by Tennessee Williams called *This Property Is Condemned*. The character I was playing was fourteen years old. I always looked young on stage. Thank God for smooth skin and great genes! It was a two-person play that took place near railroad tracks. Our director was the great Max Fisher. I loved his style. He knew how to get the best out of us. It was his description of the setting and the mindset of this fourteen-year-old that steered my performance in the right direction. Everything he said worked. I had to get into the mind of a teenager. I've always been a kid at heart, but I was a bit concerned about the role. I was worried about being a convincing fourteen-year-old. Max Fisher saw that, and before the actual debut of the play he pulled me to the side and said, "I want to talk to you."

We went out in the hall and sat on a little bench. He said, "What are you worried about?" I told him I wanted to be good. I wanted to be perfect. He said, "Look, if you weren't good, I would tell you. Just follow my direction." He was an older man who looked like he had a lot of wisdom. His eyebrows were gray and bushy; he looked like a mad scientist. He would've been a great Shakespearean actor, but his respiratory system was damaged during the Holocaust. So he chose to direct. He said, "On the day of the play, just say to yourself, 'You want to see great acting? You'll see great acting!'" So, that's what I said before I went on stage. We killed it, and the audience loved it.

Dan Freudenberger, from the Phoenix Repertory Company, was in the audience. He loved me and ask me to audition for an Off-Broadway play starring Robert Guillaume and F. Murray Abraham. This was a great break for me. I got the role. The Academy didn't allow us to take outside work, but thankfully, the head of the Academy gave me a special leave of absence. I was very grateful to her. She didn't have to do that.

MIRACLE Play was a play written by Joyce Carol Oates. It was her first play, and a black man was the lead. Robert and Murray were phenomenal. I really needed their words of encouragement. I was dealing with a hater from hell who had a small role in the play. He kept reminding that he had won an award for a commercial he had done and that he'd already been in umpteen plays, and blah, blah, blah. He wanted me to give him my role. He suggested that I tell the Company that I didn't feel up to handling it and that he was better qualified for the role. Then I would take his small role because it was better suited for me. I was already intimidated by the great talent of Robert and Murray. I really didn't need this nonsense as a distraction.

He'd say, "Look, man, nothing against you, but you shouldn't have this part. I should have this part. You haven't paid any dues. I've been acting since I was in my mother's womb. I won this award and that award. This isn't you. You shouldn't have this part." I started to believe him for a minute, and I didn't feel I was worthy of the part. But that didn't last long. Haters come in all races and genders. There will always be those who seek to tear you down. But it's not about that. It's about what God has for you. One day Robert Guillaume overheard my hater at work. He said, "Leave the kid alone." He respected Robert enough to shut up and never bother me again. The best revenge was the great review I got from *Daily News Entertainment* journalist Kathleen Carroll. The best revenge is success. That's the best way to shut the haters down.

A good friend from ISU came to see the play one night with his wife. This was his first time seeing me act. I was so happy with my review that I was on a supernatural high. I couldn't wait to hear what my friend thought. I was in the dressing room waiting for him to tell me how great I was, and he said: "I saw it. That ain't you. This isn't something you should pursue. I didn't like it. I'm saying this as your friend. I don't think this acting thing is working out for you." I looked at him with the focus and intensity of an eagle so that he'd know I wasn't playing with him. Then I said, "Take it back!" He said, "Huh?" I said, "Huh, my ass! Take back what you said or leave. Ain't no in-between. I don't want to have a discussion on it either. Take it back or leave—that simple." He'd always known me to be a people pleaser, always joking around. I kept staring and waiting. Then he said, "OK, I take it back. I'm sorry." I said, "OK, no problem." The three of us—he, his wife, and I—went out to dinner afterwards, and ended our evening on a good note. However, I still excommunicated him.

Don't be fooled by a forced or false apology. A person giving that type of apology is lying, and he or she will do more damage if allowed to remain in your circle. A verbal apology is not necessarily a sincere one. Either you're with the dream or you're not. If not, you stay in your neighborhood, and I'll stay in mine. Just know that God has me on a mission, so I want to be able to see it until I achieve it.

I hugged my friend and wished him well. But when he called, I'd say "I'm busy." Some people are in our lives only for a season and others for a lifetime. Don't mistake the seasonal friends for the lifers. But what do you do when opposition to the dream comes from your mother, husband or wife, or a close sister or brother? You can't excommunicate your mother. So what do you do? Pray.

I was often depressed after my Mom's phone calls because she didn't see the dream. One day God put something in my heart to tell her. I said, "Didn't you tell me that no one can love me like Jesus?" She paused and looked at me as if to say where is this going? Then she agreed that she had said it. I said, "So, I'm telling you that Jesus put it in my heart to pursue acting. And only Jesus knows what's best for me because He created me. In a thousand lifetimes, Mom, you could never love me like Jesus does. I could never know what's best for me like he knows. You and Grandma and Elder Chandler taught me that all my life. So please, Mom, just love me. Even if you don't agree with my decision, don't say anything negative about it. Just pray for me." And we were good. Mom never said anything negative about my decision again. I had a few other friends that I had to give the talk to, but when they persisted to be negative and did not take my career choice seriously, I had to cut them off. God loves me more.

You will never be successful waiting on permission from someone else to pursue your dream. God has the final say. That doesn't mean I don't listen to pastors, prophets, or evangelists. I belong to West Angeles COGIC. I love Bishop Blake and his teachings. I feel the presence of God in him. And I know he would tell you the same as I: "EXPECT A MIRACLE."

Shortly after my run with *Miracle Play* had ended, auditions were being held for a play called *Thieves,* starring Marlowe Thomas. Gloria Dolan was over the Green Room at the Academy, and she assisted student with getting agents. She called an agent and asked him if he'd ever heard of Ernest Thomas. He hadn't, so she said, "That's the last time you'll say that!" The agent wanted to know if I could play a twelve-year-old boy. I said it would be a stretch, but I'd try. The agent was excited about my having the nerve to try it. The director was the late Michael Bennett, who created and directed *A Chorus Line* and *Dreamgirls.* I walked onto the stage wearing jeans and a t-shirt. I bent over a little so I would appear to be shorter. Everyone started laughing. Mike said, "Ernest, do you know how old this character is supposed to be?" I said, "Yes!" He said, "Do you know he's supposed to be twelve years old?" I said in the youngest-sounding voice I could muster, "Yes." He asked, "How old are you?" In that same voice, I answered, "Twelve." He came to the stage and shook my hand. He said, "We're looking for a shorter twelve, but you're going to make it, Ernest. You had the guts to come in here and audition for the part. You're going to make it." I thanked him for that. Haywood Nelson, who played Dwayne on *What's Happening!!*, got the part of the twelve-year-old boy.

Then Gloria connected me with another agent, and I auditioned for a musical starring Bette Davis, called *The Corn Is Green*. My friend Dorian Harewood was already cast in it. I went and sang two songs I knew. I borrowed the sounds and styles of Frank Sinatra and Sammy Davis, Jr. and acted out the songs. I sang *Feelin' Good* and *I Gotta Be Me*, a cappella. The great Joshua Logan was the director. He came to the stage and said, "Great, Ernest. Can you dance?" I said, "No." One thing I've learned in this business is that you never say no. You just go out and learn what is needed. But I didn't know that then. "Oh, you gotta dance," he said. The agent was furious. He later asked me, "Why would you say something so stupid? Always say you can do it. They were going to give you the job." When I saw an overdue phone bill on his desk as I was leaving, I understood his anger. I was his ticket to getting the phone bill paid.

Gloria got me another agent, the Fifi Oscard Agency. They were awesome. I had heard about this new play titled *Don't Call Back* that Tony Perkins was directing. They were looking for more thuggish-looking Black men to audition for the role of the gang leader. The agency hadn't submitted me for an audition. I didn't know if they were having trouble getting me in, or if they didn't think I was right for the part, so I went to the producer's office myself. There was a sign on the door saying "No solicitation." But, you know what I did? I knocked on the door and put on that face my mom couldn't resist. The producer opened the door with fire in his eyes, "Don't you see the sign? — 'NO SOLICITATION.'" I put on that face and said "I'm so sorry." He said, "OK, come on in. You don't look like a gang leader. You got a baby face. We're looking at good candidates. If we can't find anyone, we'll let you know." That was promising to me because I was believing that role was mine.

I knew I had to get ready for this role. I had to come off tough and believable. My imagination kicked in at around five in the morning, and I came up with a monologue that would be perfect for the character. I got my black tape recorder. You know the big, bulky one that you can't find anymore? Someone borrowed mine and never return it. (You know who you are!) Anyway, at about five thirty that morning, the monologue was done.

The story is about a drug dealer who lives with his mother. She finds some drugs and puts them in the toilet. He doesn't know it, but he knows the drugs aren't where he left them. I wrote the monologue down, acted it out many times, and memorized it, and I was ready. I anticipated them being mesmerized by my performance. But I needed to overcome one obstacle — my baby face. I had to get people to see me as a threat. I remembered my cousins who were in a gang, and I put some of that to use. I knew the threat had to be in my eyes and voice, because I had a baby face. I decided I'd put on a black t-shirt and jeans.

The following night I went to 81st and Columbus Avenue, which was a grocery store. Next to it was a doorway to a vacant building. My goal was to stare people down and make them look away. If I could make people look away and fear me, the role was mine. I mainly focused on my cousin Sidney for inspiration. I remembered how he came to our apartment that Saturday with a gun and made my stepfather beg for his life. That entire episode was paying off. Actors use everything we can to make our role authentic. I remembered his walk, his eyes, his spirit. I was getting high just thinking about it. Tonight would be the test. So I stood in front of the building, staring everyone down. Success! Everyone looked away. Well, you know there's always one person who will try you. So, a White guy, between fifty and sixty, came by. I stared him down, and he stared back at me, smoking a cigarette. He comes and stands next to me and says, "Nice night" or something like that. I said, "What the..! Get the ... out my face!" He moved away from me and took out a switchblade. "Who the ... you think you talking to?" he said. Now, truth be told, when I saw that switchblade, my heart was about to beat out of my chest. But I couldn't show that. I refused to show weakness. I got louder: "M**f**r!, use it. Use it! Use it!" I said, screaming at the top of my lungs. Then he ran away. "GOTCHA!" I said. I was confident I would get the part.

Before going to the audition, I bought a pocket knife with a leather strand. I was going to have it in my hand for my monologue. They were mesmerized by my performance.

My agents were excited because the producers wanted me to audition for Tony Perkins. I went in with the intention of doing the same thing, but I was extremely nervous because I idolized Tony Perkins. I blew the audition. It was so embarrassing. The producers asked Tony to give me another chance because they were impressed with what I had just done before. The next time I rocked it, and Tony was very pleased.

The final audition would be a reading with the casting director. I wanted that role so badly that I got up enough nerve to ask the new head of the Academy, Mike Thomas, if he would coach me. I had been in a play directed by him before, and he had taught me "less is more." We went over the scene, and Mike directed me to perfection. When we were done, he looked at me with conviction and certainty and said, "Do it just like we rehearsed, and you'll get the role."

I couldn't wait to audition. I went in and did just what Mike had told me. I felt at one with the character. Later, my agent called and told me I had gotten the part. I ran to Mike's office to tell him I had gotten it. When I did, he looked at me and said, "I know, I know."

I booked another high-profile audition with the king of producers, Hal Prince. And I was hired to be in three plays under the Phoenix Repertory Company. I got two bookings at the same time. The head agent, Fifi herself, came to meet me, and I signed a contract with the agency. Up to that time, I guess they wanted to see if I had the goods. Fifi said, "You're the man of the hour."

Fifi and Howard Askenase worked it out where I could do both roles because they happened at different times. *Don't Call Back* was first. I was contracted to star in the opening at Falmouth Playhouse, in Falmouth, Massachusetts. Then I had the option to continue with the play on Broadway or go with Hal Prince. The supernatural feels so good; it's almost too good to be true. But it is true. You might pinch yourself a few times and find it difficult to sleep because you want to stay awake and enjoy it twenty-four/seven, but it's real.

Tony Perkins told me that if he were in my shoes he would stay with the play and go to Broadway. He said he was a little more ambitious. The beautiful Arlene Francis was staring in the play. She took me aside and asked me personally to come with her to Broadway to play the role. I was torn because I also wanted to work with Hal Prince. I ended up choosing to work with Hal Prince. The multi-talented Dorian Harewood took that role and won an award for it.

Rehearsals with Hal Prince took place at the Helen Hayes Theater. Helen Hayes is considered the first lady of the theater. She gave us our Associate of Arts certificates at graduation. What an honor!

The Phoenix Repertory subscribers were more excited about the play *The Member of the Wedding* than the other two plays. I played the role of Honey Camden Brown, a trumpet player. It had been a Broadway hit for two years in the 1950s, starring Julie Harris, Ethel Waters, Brandon De Wilde, and James Edwards. Marge Eliot took on the monumental task of bringing Berenice Sadie Brown, made famous by Ethel Waters, to life, and Mary Beth Hurt had the role of Frankie Addams, made famous by Julie Harris.

I wasn't good with money back then. I spent it as soon as I made it. I got a one-bedroom apartment in New York Central Park West for eight hundred dollars a month, which was a lot of money back then. I had never been taught how to invest money or save it for a rainy day. I lived in the moment.

I had a roommate named Scotty. He had also been a student at the Academy, but he wasn't selected for the second year. He worked and helped pay the rent. After the plays, the money dried up. I had no money saved, so I relied on my unemployment checks. My unemployment benefits didn't last very long, so Scotty got nervous and moved out. A few months later, I was forced to do the same.

During my last year in New York, I had four deaths in a row in my circle—my uncle, Jake's sister Dot, my cousin Herman, and the most difficult one of all, my grandmother. I heard a voice tell me Dot was dead during our tour of *The Member of the Wedding*. While eating with Marge between shows one day, a voice whispered and said "Dot is dead." And I said out loud, "DOT IS DEAD." Marge asked me how I knew. I told her I'd just heard it. Members of the cast all looked at me like I was having a mental breakdown. I said, "I gotta call Jake!"

When I called, I got no answer. There was no answer at Ivory's place either, and that's when I knew it was true. Jake finally called me and said Dot was dead. I said, "I know. I heard it while sitting with the other actors." We just connected like that.

Jake never talked about God. It wasn't that he didn't believe. He just never discussed the subject. I couldn't go to all those funerals, but I had to go to my grandmother's. It was hard. I would come to visit, but after she had a stroke, my visits got fewer. I hated seeing her confined to a bed like she was. It did something to me. I had always seen her as a strong woman, working around the house and singing with her Mahalia Jackson records. My grandmother was everything to me. It was difficult to take in. She was the first one to teach me about Jesus and God, and she was the first person to take me to church. She never let anyone hit me, ever. I admit it; she spoiled me rotten.

My brother, Anton, took her passing really hard. He tried to jump in the casket with her. I didn't cry. I had to be strong for everyone else. But when I was alone, I cried.

I remember Grandma and the things she said to me. I remember how excited I was when I first got on Broadway. I called my mother and said, "Mom I'm on BROADWAY!" And without missing a beat, she said: "Broadway and what, sugar? I'll come pick you up." They didn't get it. They had no concept of Broadway or its importance to an actor. My grandmother got on the phone and asked, "When you gonna get on television, baby?" I said, "I don't know." And Grandma said, "Don't worry. One day you'll be on television." That was so profound. Anything Grandma spoke about my future was prophetic to me. I never forgot that moment.

I called my one ally, Jake, and told him that I was going to Hollywood to get my own TV show. Jake, of course, was in total agreement. I was setting my sights onward and upward to the next supernatural zone.

CHAPTER FOUR

HOLLYWOOD

When I saw the movie *Cooley High* at a theater in Chicago with Jake and some friends, I was upset because I wasn't in the role of Leroy "Preach" Jackson, which was played to perfection by the great Glynn Turman. I never talk while watching a movie, but this was different. I felt I had a righteous cause. I felt I had gotten robbed. Jake thought it was amusing because throughout the film I would say, "That's my role." My agent said Hollywood hires black actors already in Hollywood. All roads were leading to California. I knew *Cooley High* was a done deal, but I wanted to go to Hollywood to get on television, specifically to have my own TV show. My agent told me she'd give me six months before I'd be back in New York. I loved Fifi Oscard, and the agency did bless me early on in my career. But when she said that, I said to myself, "You have been excommunicated."

Fifi was kind enough to give me a list of agents. But what good was that when she was saying I'd be back in six months because I wouldn't make it.

After losing four loved-ones, being evicted from my apartment, and missing the chance to act in *Cooley High,* it was time to make a bold move. I needed money. I received help from a local church called The Little Church Around the Corner. They gave me 200 dollars more than they had ever given anyone who was not a member of the church. The Actors Fund also gave me about 200 dollars. I needed money for a redeye flight to Hollywood. I even visited a Synagogue, where a Rabbi gave me words of encouragement. He said he felt something good about me and encouraged me to pursue my dream. We ate some bread that was swirled like huge dreadlocks. I felt I was one step closer to my dream.

Of course, Jake continued to encourage me to follow my dream. So, I packed my bags and bought a one-way ticket to Hollywood. When you're going into the supernatural zone, burn your ship. I didn't plan on returning to New York in defeat six months later, as my agent had predicted. As Joel Osteen says, "Man doesn't have the final say; God has the final say." You may feel vulnerable, isolated, and lonely, but tell your Creator all about it. Don't cry to a living soul. Trust me. You will cry at night, but joy will come in the morning.

My old roommate Scotty wrote me a beautiful poem. He told me to read it on the plane. After I got in my seat, I read it. I couldn't believe Scotty saw me like that. I don't remember the entire poem, but I do remember him saying, "Ernie is next to God." I believe he meant my faith was strong. I was making a

bold move that was bringing me closer to God and strength-
ening my faith. I had bought a plant for my grandmother's
funeral, but I didn't leave it there. I wanted to take it with me.
I knew she was still rooting for me. While sitting there on the
plane, I said, "God, you said ask anything in your name. I want
my own television show, with a positive role. I will always give
you glory."

Speak the dream. Speak what you want, and be clear about
it. Believe it as truth, and it will come to pass, in Jesus' name.

When I arrived in Hollywood, I didn't have a permanent
place to stay, but friends had referred me to a few of their relatives. I stayed with Ivory's sister-in-law and her husband for
about a week or so. They had just gotten married. I felt like
a third wheel, but they were nice. I knew her sister Brenda,
who was Ivory's wife, very well, and that's why I felt comfortable being there. Brenda was like a sister to me. Ivory was my
blood brother in my mind. I thank God for blessing me with his
friendship.

I met two good guys, and we became friends immediately. Marcus Hunter was a writer. He'd just completed a book
titled *Throwaway Child*. And Moose was a funny Jewish comedian. Moose never wore socks. The first advice he gave me was,
"Ernie, you gotta get "F#@&K YOU" money, and then you will
be free and not give a damn about Hollywood hiring you or
not, and you won't get so anxious at auditions."

He introduced me to Lenny Bruce's mother by phone, and
she was extremely encouraging. What a sweet lady. I heard she
had encouraged a lot of people. The late comedian Sam Kinison

said she was very encouraging to him at a time when people didn't like his style of comedy. God bless Sally forever.

I had many hungry days, but I never starved. The trick was buying Snickers® candy bars. They fill you up and cut your appetite. Of course, there are healthier options today. Don't try to live off Snickers® bars! There were some cheap restaurants in the area. One was South Town, in Hollywood. You could get eggs, sausage, toast, and coffee for $1.99.

I had the list of agents, but no guarantees. Rejection, rejection, rejection — nine rejections in a row. I had to regroup. By this time, I had found a cheap hotel for thirty-five dollars a week — the Gilbert Hotel on Wilcox, between Sunset and Hollywood. One day I had an emotional moment where I just screamed and started banging on the hotel walls. Nine rejections in a row. I thought about what Fifi had said about coming back in six months. Then I just cried out to God. I cried until my head hurt. I literally cried myself to sleep that night. But I didn't give up. I remembered that Jesus doesn't lie. I had asked for a television show in Jesus' name. I knew it was going to happen, but I didn't feel it that night. You don't have to always feel godly and super positive, but you have to always act as if what you asked for is about to happen. You can't always trust your feelings. Feelings are traitors to the soul.

Each morning I showered, put on a nice suit and cologne, and prayed to God. Then I was out the door, looking clean, dressed for success. While at the beach one day, I met Richard Castellano, who played the role of Peter Clemenza in *The Godfather*. He said, "Ernest Thomas is a strong name." That really blessed me.

After being rejected by nine agents, there was only one left—Tom Korman. I believe you have to live each day as if it's your last. When you do, you go into the supernatural zone, and the universe is at your command and at your service. I dare you to live each day as if it's your last. You will be amazed at the blessings that come to fruition. Every second is an opportunity to achieve what you want your reality to be. And God gives us favor because we appreciate every breath of life, every second of life. God honors that. He rewards gratitude.

When it seems all paths to the dream are fading, it is sometimes amazing what can be spoken—the right things to say, things we never thought of. We become a magnet, attracting everything that will make the dream a reality.

When I went to see Tom Korman, I said to him, "Look, Mr. Korman. If I don't act, I am gonna die." Tom looked at me and smiled. He said, "I believe you." So he got on the phone and called the top casting director, Jan Murry, who was primarily casting for sitcoms at that time. She worked with *All in the Family*, *The Jeffersons*, *Good Times*, *Sanford and Son*, *Maude*— you name it. Bud Yorkin and Norman Lear were the kings of producing. The top eight shows on TV were theirs. My first audition was for *Grady*. This was a spin-off of *Sanford and Son*. When I arrived for the audition, Bud Yorkin said, "This is the situation. You're here to date Grady's granddaughter. Go for it." I remembered a friend of mine who lied all of the time. He would say that he was related to Johnny Mathis and some other celebrities. We knew he was lying, but he never backed down. I decided to draw from him for inspiration for the audition. I said something like, "I want to date your granddaughter.

I can introduce you to my cousin Johnny Mathis, and Sidney Poitier—he's my father." I just went with it and let it flow. I will say this; Bud Yorkin laughed so hard that snot came out of his nose. My performance made Whitman Mayo laugh, too. I didn't get the role. I don't know if they even did that particular episode.

Then I auditioned for a part on *The Jeffersons*. I loved that show! I got booked. By the time I got home, I had gotten a call. Jake was the first one I called. He said, "I told you!" So I took a bus to CBS Studios on Fairfax, in Los Angeles. This is where they shot the show. Jack Shea, the director, took me around to meet the whole cast. When we got to Sherman Hemsley, he wouldn't shake my hand. He glanced at me and then looked back at his script. Jack said, "This is Ernest Thomas." Sherman said, "So what, Ernest?" Actually, I was glad he did that because it made me work harder. I didn't take it for granted that I would be great. I thought I needed to prove something to Sherman. But during rehearsal, he never said anything about my performance at all.

I went to the director and said, "Man, what's going on?" He told me not to worry about Sherman. Damon Evans and Isabel Sanford were great. Isabel even gave me a ride home that day. Her cousin often drove her to the studio, and they came by the Gilbert Hotel and picked me up every day while I was working on the show. She was a real sweetheart.

On the episode I was in, I played a thief who steals George's company van while he is doing a speech at a youth center. My character's name was Train, and I was a childhood friend of Lionel's, played by Damon Evans. The audience loved me. They laughed in all the right places. Again, when you can make that connection with the character, the audience is with you. They have bought into the lie. It's a high that's better than sex.

When the announcer introduced me at the end of the show, he introduced me as Ernest Thompson. Sherman Hensley ran out in front of the curtain and told the announcer, "His name is Ernest Thomas! He's going to be a huge star!" Sherman pulled me to the side and told me, "You need to watch out for the energy vampires (people that drain your energy and have nothing to add to your life)." And of course he mentioned the leeches and people who never knew me before who would now be my best friend ever! And then there are the cousins who will want to be in my life because they want money.

Then Mary White, Isabel Sanford's agent, told me that ABC was doing a new pilot called *Cooley High*. She said, "I think you will be perfect for a lead." By this time, I'm hearing the whole host of angels singing. That was the movie I wanted to be in. That's the movie I felt robbed of. Again, Glynn Turman was perfect for that role. He was supposed to have it, and I was supposed to be on television. I had wanted it badly. But just look at God!

When I told Tom that Mary White had said I would be perfect for a lead role in *Cooley High*, Tom got upset. He said, "Tell that bitch to stay away from my client. I already know about the audition. I'm setting it up right now."

When I arrived for the audition, I saw one of the producers on the lot reading a newspaper. I could tell he really liked me and thought I should get the lead role. Finally, my agent called and said I got the part. Jake was the first person I called when I got the news. He said, "I told you."

We shot the pilot in Los Angeles. People always ask where we shot the show. I forget to bring up Chicago. Initially, they were trying to keep the title *Cooley High.* So they wanted to keep some of it in Chicago. We shot most of the scenes in Los Angeles and some of the outside scenes in Chicago. Ivan Dixon was the director. Garrett Morris, who played the role of the teacher in the movie, also played the role in the pilot. Maurice Marshall, who played Damon in the movie, also played that role in the pilot. They were the only two originals from the film that were in the TV cast. Carla Kilpatrick played the role of Dee. Danielle Spencer auditioned, but didn't get the part. Cochise was played by Dorian Harewood, and Dorothy Meyer was cast as Shirley.

Jake was there when we shot the pilot. I was so happy that Jake could see the dream come to fruition. In one scene, we were running up the stairs. I fell on the steps, which were made of steel. My knee started swelling, and we still had to do a scene running through the farmer's market. Dorian and the women on the show were trying to help me doctor it. The producers were saying, "We've got to shoot this scene. We have a budget here." I was hoping for a little mercy, but I did understand. Dorian came up with the idea of doing a little dance routine. He made up the routine so that I could hop through the farmer's market, grabbing the fruit. Arnold Margolin one of the producers loved it. God bless Dorian. After watching the pilot, ABC decided not to pick up the show. That was a sad day. I remember talking on the phone with Arnold. He said, "Look, Ernest, your efforts were monumental. Keep the tape so you can get other jobs." I didn't heed his advice.

Shortly after that, I met Leon. He was a pimp, but not one you'd see hanging around on the street. He was a nice guy. We became friends, and started hanging out together. That's when I first started using drugs. I laughed about everything. Food tasted so good with weed. The thing about weed is you never hear of the user robbing anyone, beating anyone, or going postal. I'm just saying. I had a lot of fun on weed. I even said this recently when I won the outstanding Christian award. I also spoke about the pimps and prostitutes who had been some of my best supporters. They never gave up on me. The Christians were pointing fingers and basically calling me a looser. The pimps and prostitutes didn't say if you ask God in Jesus' name it's done. They just believed.

CHAPTER FIVE

WHAT'S HAPPENING

In the summer of '75, after the *Cooley High* pilot was rejected, the producers called my agent and said they had decided to fire the entire previous cast and cast new people around me. I thought they were just trying to let me down easy. I didn't think it could be true. But it turned out it was true. This time they were planning to use three cameras instead of one. I thought that was a big deal. They auditioned a lot of people, and I would come to the auditions. One guy was like a Black Jerry Lewis. He totally upstaged me. I felt like I was invisible when he was around. I just knew this guy was going to get my part. I thought the producers were going to tell me I was fired. I was believing every day would be my last. I went in to talk to them after his audition. I told them that I didn't see Preach Jackson as a street guy. I saw him as a guy who could be any race. Any guy would want him as a best friend; any teacher would choose him as a favorite student. They just looked at me as if I were crazy and said thank you for sharing.

It turned out that they didn't want the "Black Jerry Lewis."
I was, indeed, chosen for the part. That's when I met the rest of
the cast. It's very seldom, if ever, that you walk into a room and
instantly connect with everyone in the room. But that's what
happened when I met the cast for the show. All of them were
there — Mable King, Shirley Hemphill, Fred Berry, Haywood
Nelson, and Danielle Spencer. From the moment we shook
hands, it was surreal. We knew we were a family. It was like
reuniting with loved ones we'd known for years. And that's
how it always was. We really loved each other.

I was cast as the lead. That prayer on the plane had become a reality. I had asked for it. We were all going to be stars.
I was in the supernatural zone. I needed to pinch myself. What
had seemed impossible was not only possible; it had become
reality.

The first couple of weeks were spent rehearsing for the
pilot. During that time, we took breaks together and hung out
together. When we shot the pilot, the audience loved us. After
the show, the producers, Bud, Saul, and Bernie walked me to
my car. They said, "Ernie, don't get your hopes up. They shoot
hundreds of pilots, and most don't make it. I said, "Yes, but
God is on our side." I remember the pimp that I had met while
shooting the pilot. He really believed that I would make it. He
jumped on top of the car, shouting, "We're stars!" It was something magical. We just knew it would be a hit.

When asked how the name of the show got changed from
Cooley High to *What's Happening!!*, I tell people there are two
versions of that story — the way I remember it happening, and
the way Haywood remembers it. According to Haywood,

he suggested that we call the show *What Happening!!* Every time I hear him tell his version, I shake my head and tell him I don't remember that. The way I remember it is quite different. Back then, whenever we greeted one another, we'd say, "What's happening?" And that's how it came to be the title of the show, because we were always saying it. At any rate, it was Bud Yorkin's decision to make, and so the show was officially changed to *What's Happening!!*

After the name change, we were also allowed to change the names of our characters. I chose Roger, Raj for short. When I was in New York, I had stayed at the Roger Williams. So I chose it for good luck, not realizing until years later, while being interviewed by a reporter from India, that Raj means emperor, or someone of royalty. Danielle chose Dee, and Haywood chose Dwayne. Mabel, Shirley, and Fred kept their names. Fred got the nickname Rerun because he was always repeating grades in school.

I was twenty-five years old playing the role of a sixteen-year-old. Thanks to my good genes and slender frame, I was able to pull it off. But I've always been a kid and heart, and I still am. I welcomed the opportunity to play a teenager; I actually relished it. As a sheltered, super-spoiled kid, it was easy to be Raj. I've always had a strong imagination, so it wasn't hard to lose myself in the character. It was euphoric, in the sense that I could go back to a space in time when life was easier. And I found myself staying there, even when the lights and cameras were off. I had fallen so in love with being Roger that it was hard to "turn him off." Finally, my brother said to me one day, "Ernie, can you come back to being Ernest. Can I have Ernest, please?" It was then that I realized just how deep into the character I had gone.

As the show progressed and we did more episodes, we were spending more time together. During this time, Danielle starting tying to really make me her big brother. And I told her, "Ok, little girl, you're *acting* as my sister, and I'm *acting* as your brother. We're not really brother and sister. I like you, and we have fun. But then you go your way, and I go mine." She looked at me as if to say, "What a butt hole!" But she'd always be right there every time I turned around. One day she just wasn't taking it any more. She literally scratched me up that day. I was bleeding. I looked at her in bewilderment, and I remember saying, "What's wrong with this kid? She's lost her mind." And Shirley said, "She loves you, fool!" And that's when it clicked for me. I didn't get it at first.

After that, Danielle was around all the time. She would hang out at my place any time — both she and Haywood. They were the youngest members of the cast. He was fifteen, and she was nine. They looked up to me as their big brother. And I really started to enjoy and appreciate that. It reminded me of what a blessing it is to have someone love you like that.

Danielle and her stepfather were in a terrible accident during the second year of the show. We were in the emergency room waiting to hear if she had lived or died. Shirley was crying, and the rest of us were in a state of shock. The doctor came out and said he had good and bad news. The bad news was Danielle's stepfather had died from his injuries. The good news was Danielle survived, but she was in critical condition. It was a little rocky for her for a time, but she bounced back through her faith and with a strong mother, grandmother, and great-grandmother by her side.

Haywood and Dee were the brainiacs. They were very smart as well as talented. Haywood was always doodling, and he's always been great with words. He was the heartthrob of the show. Every time he was introduced in front of the live audience, the women would go crazy, screaming for him. He was shy and never took it seriously. My brother Anton was staying with me during that time, and he and Haywood became very close friends.

Although Thalmus Rasulala was only playing the role of my father on the show, it still meant a lot to me personally because, during those moments of make believe, I had a father. Even off the set, he treated me as if I were his son. During his first entrance as our father on the show, he hugged me and kissed me on the cheek. He meant nothing by it; he was just acting like a father who hadn't seen his son since he was a little boy. But that made me uncomfortable and want to push him away because I had never had a father. He even apologized when he saw my reaction. I didn't understand where he was coming from. His wife told me years later, "If anyone ever loved you, it was my husband." But at the time I didn't know. Again, I didn't get it. Sometimes people don't want anything from you but just you. They're just naturally drawn to the essence of you, and that connection is real and even divine.

Shirley and I were great friends. We used to hang out from time to time, but Shirley hated giving autographs. She thought her performance on television was enough. If we were out eating or socializing, she was irritated when fans approached us, and it angered her when I would give autographs. She once said to me, "You make me sick," because I kept signing autographs during our lunch and even as we walked back to our cars. So we agreed to stop hanging out so she could be true to who she was and I could be true to who I was, because I didn't mind signing autographs at all.

Shirley was extremely funny. She had a wicked sense of humor. I would often attend her shows when she did stand-up, and I would laugh so hard. I wasn't acting. I love stand-up comedy, and she was just that funny to me. But she wanted me to stop coming because she thought others would think that we'd planned it, and she wanted to see if she could make others laugh on her own. She thought I was biased. I thought she was hilarious.

Shirley was the voice of reason on the show. She spoke her mind, and she told it like it was. I remember times when I would get serious and deep about the show. I took my craft seriously. Shirley would say to me, "Ease up, Pachino. It's a sitcom. Don't be so serious." And she was right. As the show continued to become more and more successful, Shirley would have to speak to the egos. She would say, "Ernest is the star of the show." I would sort of cringe because she would say it to both Fred and Mable. I knew she meant well, but I didn't want any hard feelings between us. But Shirley was a sweetheart. She was always guarded and aloof. I think she just didn't want to be hurt or disappointed. I knew she carried a lot past hurts and pain, but she was strong, and she was one of my dearest friends.

Mable was a very talented actress. When I saw her that first day on the set I was star struck. I told her I had seen her in *The Wiz* on Broadway fifteen times. She gave a supernatural performance as Evilene, the wicked witch. She was so awesome that they cast her in the same role for the movie version.

She and I developed a good relationship. She could be somewhat overbearing at times, and that's when we would bump heads. She had somewhat of a following during that time. Many young actors and actresses looked up to her as their mentor and mother figure. She would have group sessions at her house, and she tried on many occasions to get me to join in, but I never did.

At the end of the second season, the producers decided that they wanted to focus mainly on the guys and scale Mable's character back to about five out of the twenty-six episodes. The negotiations between the producers and her agent went awry, and they refused to meet her demands. I was very sad to see it end that way. She was such a great talent.

Fred and I were like brothers. He wasn't really an actor, but he got better as time went on. He was an awesome dancer, and he was part of a dance group called The Lockers. He used to tell me how it bothered him that The Lockers were jealous of him because he had gotten a role on the show and had become very popular. After getting them on an episode of the show, that seemed to help his relationship with the group, which I know meant a lot to him.

Our dressing rooms were not in the best condition when we first started the show. They were far below the standards of what TV stars should have. And after the second season, Fred and I decided to ask the producers for better dressing rooms and a salary increase. When our demands weren't met, we decided to walk off the set just before we were to perform in front of a live audience. They upgraded our dressing rooms, but we didn't get an increase. And they told us if we pulled a stunt like that again, we'd be in breach of contract. Fred and I had been drinking that day. I think it was the cognac that gave me the boldness to go through with walking off the set. I don't think I could have done it if I'd been sober.

Then the drug use started. I always tell people that whatever's in you the drugs will bring out of you. Fred became a different person when he started using drugs. As time went on, he started to change. Although he was still coming over, and we were still hanging out together, there were things that he said and did that let me know he was changing.

After the walkout, he still didn't seem happy with the show. It was if he was trying to sabotage it. Every week he was stirring up something with the producers. He'd come on the set late. And he really started to think that he was the star and that the show wouldn't make it without him. That's why they started replacing Fred's character with a character called Snake. They were doing that to try to shake Fred up. And that did seem to calm him down a bit. He was really shaken when they found a guy who looked exactly like him. They had him wear baggy pants, suspenders, and a beret, and sit in the front row of the audience during the show. Then they would point him out at each show and say, "Oh, wow! This guy looks just like Rerun. What do you want to be?" And the guy would say, "I want to be Rerun." And they'd say, "Wow! We already have a Rerun, but thank you!" That used to freak Fred out.

Then there were times when Fred seemed to be acting as if he was jealous of me. After I had others come to me and share things that he had said about me, it made me very uncomfortable to be alone with him. He'd still come over to my house to hang out, so I just made sure that I wasn't alone with him when he did.

Even in our third season, Fred was attempting to undermine the show. The producers called a meeting with the cast because Fred had called and told them that we thought they were racist. At the meeting, we tried to explain that we didn't feel that way at all. But there was no use denying it. Fred made it seem to them as if we were backtracking on what we'd said. So the producers said, "Well, we don't want you working for racists. And Fred would never back down or admit that he'd lied. He kept insisting throughout the meeting that we felt that way. Looking back on it, these men were Jewish, and the last thing they wanted to be called was racist. I know it hurt them to think we felt that way. I was furious with Fred for doing that.

But my mother thought Fred could do no wrong. She wouldn't let anyone say anything negative about him. And Fred's mother loved me. She thought I could do no wrong. Our families got along well. My brother and sister loved Fred, too. But there were many things that Fred did that people couldn't forgive him for. There were many broken promises, lots of misdeeds. But my mother always defended him. She'd always say, "You don't know what a person has been through." I always felt that Fred had his demons that he struggled with, and he just couldn't overcome them.

Before he died, he asked for my forgiveness, and I gave it to him. And I knew he'd be gone soon. His son asked me to officiate his funeral, and I agreed to do it. There were many who didn't agree with my decision to even attend his funeral, let alone eulogize him. But his son had asked, and I loved Fred — the Fred without the drugs.

People have asked me how I felt about the writing on the show. At the time, I wished we (the cast) could have been more involved. As a whole, I was fine with the writing. There was just one word that I had a problem with: "gee." I told the producers I'd never heard a black kid use that word. But the producers would say, "Well, Ernie, we want to appeal to mainstream America." At the time, I did wish they had allowed us to come up with scenarios for the show. But the show has stood the test of time without us doing that. It was the characters that the world fell in love with. It was our job to make the characters who they were, and the fans loved us. The great and incomparable Tupac Shakur, Will Smith, Allen Iverson, and Dr. Maya Angelou are just a few of those fans who have expressed their love over the years. There's not a day that goes by that I'm not shown love for the joy we have brought into the lives of people through the show. When I'm out in public, and people want my autograph or a picture, or they run up to me and hug me, they can say the lines verbatim. To them, everything we said was gold.

One of my favorite episodes of the show is "Doobie or Not Doobie" (Parts 1 and 2). That was our only two-part episode.

The fans' favorite line from that show is "Which Doobie you be?" When they told us the Doobie Brothers would be on the show, I really didn't know who they were referring to. But when they came on the set and started rehearsing for the show, then I thought, *"Ohhhhh! I know that song! Oh, man! Now I get it."* They were amazing guys, so nice and down to earth. And I liked the fact that we were pushing the envelope and having these long-haired White rockers on the show. I loved the fact that they were an interracial group with a sound that was about to take them to the next level. And I knew they would bring more attention to the show.

We had some really good times with the band. Michael McDonald even invited us to his house. So we would go over and hang out. We had lots of fun, and the music was great. He had a spectacular house, and when I found out he had built another one just like it for his mother, I had even more respect for him. I thought it was so cool of him to take care of his mother in that way.

I also like the episode "My Three Tons." That's the episode Fred got his dance group, The Lockers, on. I like this episode because it has a moral. The dancers wanted Rerun to join their group just so they could make fun of him because he was overweight. But when Dwayne finds this out, Mama devises a plan to get back at the group. I especially like episodes like this one because there are teachable moments there, where Mama is able to share her wisdom, making the episode impactful and meaningful.

I also like "The Hospital Stay." In this episode, the wisdom comes through Dee. She's talking to the patient in the hospital who hasn't spoken to his daughter in years because she married a White man. And Dee asks him which one? That was profound, in the sense that she was saying that's silly. "You're mad because she married a White man?" And here she's teaching him. So, again, we're dealing with moral issues and addressing relevant topics.

I also like the two episodes about Raj being interested in older women. They show that he is a silly romantic like me, always trying to make the lady laugh. I especially like the episode "The Landlady" because it is heartbreaking. It gave me a chance to express those gray areas. Raj has to show that it doesn't bother him when she arrives with this handsome guy, which he finds out is her fiancé. Up to this point, he has been thinking there was something romantic and meaningful developing between them. And then he discovers that the surprise is not that he and the landlady will be going somewhere special alone, but instead, that she and her fiancé are taking him to the ballet. When they're leaving, Raj is laughing, but you can see that he's breaking down inside. The reveal is in what he isn't saying.

Being on *What's Happening!!* was the closest thing to heaven on earth to me. I was the happiest I'd ever been. I had gotten what I'd been praying for. The show was a huge success, and the cast was good. We had our moments, as any family does. But we did love each other, and that made it easy. I was so happy that I thought I was going to die at any moment, because life couldn't be this good. I had gotten the show, I had gotten the lead, the show was a hit, now something had to go wrong. I often thought about those who were jealous because

I had gotten the part. A lot of guys had tried out for that role. And for it to have reached the level of success that it did was a little unnerving.

I was preoccupied with thoughts of death. I knew I was going to die at any given moment. In 1977, I went to Gary, Indiana, for Ernest Thomas Day. I thought, *"Oh, God. This might be the day."* I remember being in the parade and standing up in the float, waving at people and thinking a bullet was coming any second. I was smiling and enjoying the moment, but I couldn't fight the underlying current of fear.

After the parade, I went up to the podium where they presented a bust of me. That really freaked me out. Then I knew I was dead for sure. I knew I was going to be killed that day. I was twenty-eight at the time, and I didn't think I'd live past the age of thirty-three. That was the age Jesus was when he died, so I thought that would be my final year, if I made it that far.

Seeing the bust of my head and hearing people shouting, "Touch my baby" and pushing their children or their women to be touched by me, and grabbing my hand, it was all overwhelming. It had escalated to the point where the mayor couldn't even be heard. He was trying to introduce me to the crowd, but they just wanted me, and they started to bum-rush the stage. So the security officers had to get up there, and I thought, *"Oh my goodness! They're really trying to kill me now."* The officers had to rush me off the stage and into a limousine. So then the crowd started rocking the limousine because they wanted me to get out of the limo. It was really love, but I didn't see that then. I remember my mother being really flustered. She couldn't handle it. She looked at me with this strange look on her face, as if to say, "Who are you?" It was really strange.

People often tell me, "You saved my life" or "I really loved the show" or "Thanks for the laughter" and so many other wonderful things that let me know how the show touched their lives. It was truly a supernatural experience that I will always be thankful for. As I was moving on into another season of my life, I knew deep down inside that God was not through with me, that there was more to be done. No matter how far we may drift from him, God is always there, in good times and bad—a friend that sticks closer than any brother. He truly takes care of his own. Through it all, he never left me or abandoned me. For that I will always be most grateful.

CHAPTER SIX

MALIBU

In the summer of 1977, during our hiatus from the show, I had a vision of living in a house by the water. Anton, my cousins, and I went searching for that house. We had all points from the car covered as we drove along the streets of Malibu. Then I saw the house. It was as if I heard the angels in heaven singing. What a beautiful sight! It had front double-doors that I especially liked. As soon as you entered the double doors, there was a hot tub on the left and a pool on the right. From there were more stairs leading to another set of double doors that led into the house. Once inside the house, you could see the ocean from the balcony, which was just off the living room. It was a beautiful home, with three bedrooms, a living room, and a den—simply heaven on earth.

We had so many good times and fond memories in that house. We had parties anytime—awesome parties because the music during that time was so great. It was just soulful, feel-good music. I had an open-door policy back in those days. There were no drive-by shootings, and people just wanted to hang loose and have fun. We could have a one-night stand and not die from it. We were young, Black, and independent. We were on television and living it up in Malibu. We were living the life.

Fred would often stay during the week. He had a home a few miles away, but he chose to stay at my house because it was closer to the studio, and he liked getting our friends and fans to wait on him. He was always giving orders: "Bring me a beer, or bring me this and that." Lawrence Hilton Jacobs would come up from time to time. He is an awesome pianist. He has played on some great albums, and has a few solo albums. Deniece Williams and Chaka Khan would also stop by. Who doesn't love their music? Norm Nixon, the basketball all-star would also drop in. Leon Spinks would come by from time to time. At that time, I didn't know he was a fighter. It wasn't until he later defeated Muhammad Ali that I found out. He became the heavyweight champion of the world. Who knew? At that time, we only knew that life was good, and we were sharing it with good people.

Deniece and I were dating during that time. I had a huge crush on her when we were kids. She had long, pretty pigtails and a beautiful voice, even then. There was a song called *Deep River, Lord* that she led when she sang with her choir. I'll never forget that beautiful soprano voice, so lyrical and perfect. Our success came around the same time. She had the hit *Free* and was working with Earth, Wind & Fire, and I had *What's Happening!!* So we were both at a great place in our lives.

My brother was doing his thing on the dancing scene. He was taking courses at the Inner-City Cultural Center, and he was an incredible dancer. At the dance recitals, he always received standing ovations. From modern dance, to tap, to many other styles of dance, his talent was far-reaching. He was truly in his full supernatural zone.

It was during this time that my brother revealed he was gay. Although my brother had been in several relationships with women in the past, he had always been effeminate. And, even though I accepted his lifestyle, I didn't like the type of people he was hanging with. I wanted him to be successful, and I felt that in order for him to do that, he needed to hang around successful gay people, such as doctors, accountants, and lawyers, who would keep him motivated to achieve.

Most of the friends he invited over were drama-filled drag queens, who were hilarious and fun, but they were a little over the top. There was no rumor or piece of gossip they didn't know about, and they lived to drink and party. I would look in awe at these beautiful women and handsome men, not realizing that they were gay or transgender or drag queens. My brother would shake his head. He would say to me, "You are so naïve." He brought over bi-sexual men, and they would sit in the hot tub and talk about their wives and children and then discuss their lovers. I was always shocked by what I heard. Anton would say," Excuse my brother; he knows nothing about life at all."

I must admit, I did want my brother to be more macho. I would often ask him if he really had to be so obvious with his ways. He would put his hands on his hips and use feminine gestures. But I wasn't trying to change him. My primary concern was his safety. I didn't want him to be bullied. I knew this Jamaican guy who lived in my building in New York who would boast about getting together with other guys and beating up gay men in Central Park. So I had this visual, in my very detailed imagination, of him being hurt. That never did happen, thank God. But I was always worried. I would often say to him, "I know you're gay, but can you walk more manly? You still have the man in you, right? You don't have to put this on display." It didn't dawn on me at the time that he was offended by my comments. I was really being cruel, but I didn't realize that I was.

One of the drag queens had a crush on me, but I was not having any of that. So I quickly let him know that there was no possibility of anything developing between us. And, although I had spoken to my brother about the friends that he invited over, this particular one was still coming over regularly.

One of my friends from Indiana came into town to see a boxing match and to visit his sister-in-law. We all went to the fight, and we came back to my house after we left the arena. A very popular male singer was in the bathroom getting high off of coke and liquor. When he came out of the bathroom, I introduced him to my friends, not realizing that he was high.

The famous singer was obviously feeling euphoric from the drug and the alcohol—so much so that he went over and sat between my friend and his girlfriend. He started stoking my friend's head and then his girlfriend's hair, while uttering moans and groans. They were sitting there in shock at what was happening. Then the queen with a crush on me comes strolling over and says, "Hey, Ernie, so I got that thing that you like. I'm going to fix us a meal. I know you really like it," as if something was going on between us. So then I knew my friend was thinking all sorts of crazy thoughts. But I felt he knew me, and I didn't need to address that. I didn't think I had to offer an explanation to someone who had known me for as long as he had. So I was shocked and angry when I discovered that my friend and his girlfriend had gone back to Indiana and told everyone that I was gay and having orgies at my house. Well, of course, this news spread like wildfire.

Although I could understand why my friend went back home with that type of impression, it took me years to forgive him. The Bible says that gossip is murder. When you spread things about someone that is not true, you assassinate that person's character. Several months later, I was attending a funeral, and as I was exiting the church, I overheard someone ask, "Is that Ernest Thomas?" And this young lady replied, loud enough for everyone around us to clearly hear, "Oh yeah. He's a fag."

I was really blown away by that. The same fans who were giving me mad love and adoration were now tearing me down by believing and spreading unfounded rumors and lies. Maya Angelou once said, "Those who are at your feet will soon be at your throat." Those words are so powerful and so true. Anyone who is over the top in adulation of you should be watched, because that same person can turn on you in the blink of an eye.

Later on that year I got a call from another friend in Gary. He had a friend in Los Angeles who wanted to have an art show, so he had told his friend about my place. I've always been an easy-going guy who is eager to please my friends. So, when he asked, I agreed right away — with no questions asked and no preview of the art.

On the day of the show, I met the artists, and they came in and set up their artwork. As I was watching them set up, I realized that all the artwork had one central theme—the penis and vagina. I called my friend and said, "Man, you didn't tell me that this was what the art show was about. Had I known, I wouldn't have agreed to this." But it was too late. Fliers had been out advertising the event, so there was no turning back at that point. I don't remember too much about the art show. I was high. But I do remember hearing someone say that a few celebrities came by, and there was a lot of traffic. They actually sold a lot of art that day.

Several weeks later, the artist who had put the show together and his wife invited me to an organization they belonged to. It was an organization in which businessman bought property and networked together to create wealth. Deniece, my cousin, and his wife went to the meeting with me. When we arrived, I immediately noticed a huge snake in a rectangular cage. The leader of the group was a Black man with a huge birthmark just slightly to the left of the center of his forehead. He had a beautiful wife, and their children were there. As the night went on, we could sense that something was off. They asked Deniece to sing something, so she sang "The Star-Spangled Banner." That really threw me. Out of all the songs she could have chosen, why that one? She later told me that she had chosen it to confuse the enemy, Satan.

The Bible tells us that we fight spiritual wickedness in high places, and that experience was a true testament to that fact. At the end of the meeting, Deniece, my cousin, and his wife all said goodnight and headed out the door. I stayed a little

longer because I wanted to tell them how much I appreciated
the invitation and how nice everything was, just trying to be
gracious and exchange pleasantries before leaving. But when I
attempted to turn and leave, my feet were nailed to the floor. I
looked at the couple, and their eyes were slowly moving back
and forth, from left to right. But they would not look at me. So
I kept talking, even though this was freaking me out. I really
didn't want to believe or acknowledge what I was seeing. Then,
all of a sudden, Deniece came back in and grabbed my hand
and said, "Goodnight!" And that broke the spell. I was never
so happy to see someone in my life. We sprinted to the door.
Needless to say, we never saw any of those folks again.

Almost every night was a party night at my house.
Drugs, alcohol, food, music, and dancing was the life we lived.
Although it was fun and the times were high, I was at one of the
lowest points I had ever been at in my life. I was desperate for
a lifeline. I felt like I was in the no-remedy zone, with no hope.
I had always believed in God and his presence in my life, but I
felt I was disappointing him. I knew I shouldn't have been doing the drugs, but I couldn't resist the way they made me feel; I
just couldn't shake the desire to have them.

One day my cousin came by with a guy she had been dating and was considering marrying. She wanted me to meet him.
He was Muslim, and she was Christian. When they arrived, he
was dressed in a jalabiya and kufi hat. He started talking to me
about Islam, and he started reading the Koran. We discussed
the theological differences between Islam and Christianity, and
although I didn't feel that all my questions had been fully answered, I couldn't deny how the words from the Koran brought

peace to my soul at a time when I desperately needed it. That day I took shahada, a declaration of faith. Later that day, I went walking by the water, and I was praying and thanking God for being free from the drugs. I was excited and beyond happy about my new faith.

But everyone was not happy about by new faith. In fact, most of my family and friends did not support my decision. I had Christian friends call me and tell me that I couldn't do this, that I was going to hell, and that they were very disappointed in me because I was a Muslim. Then the calls stopped. My friends no longer wanted to be bothered with me. I don't think I had anyone to say, "Well, I'll be praying for you. I love you anyway." I was completely isolated, and I literally felt hated. Although I felt alone and hurt, I refused to entertain the mockery or to respond to the attacks. I never tried to push my beliefs on anyone, but I always felt like there was a mark on my back.

I had been a Muslim for a few months before returning back to the drugs. The loneliness, the partying, and the desire for that soaring high had me caught up in the vicious cycle again. I knew only God could help me, but I also had to help myself. And yet I just couldn't shake the desire for the lady in the pipe. She comforted me and made me feel better. She did not judge me or ostracize me. She took my pain and made me feel better—only her love came at a huge price. She wanted to consume me and deceive me. And, although I knew it, I couldn't resist her. I was under her cryptic spell.

During our hiatus from the show, a friend of mine was planning to audition for Sidney Poitier's new film *A Piece of the Action.* He had asked me to help him go over his lines, and to go with him to the audition, so I did. Being in the movie had not crossed my mind. I was going just to help my friend go over his lines until it was time for him to audition. When I saw Sidney, I thought, *"Oh, my God! This is Sidney Poitier. It just doesn't get any better than this!"* I had watched all his movies, and I idolized this man. And here he was, in person.

Right before my friend's audition, Sidney asked me if I was auditioning for the movie. I told him I was there to help my friend. And he said, "Oh. You don't want to be in my movie?" And I said, "Oh, yes! Yes, I do!" He said, "Good, because I watch your show." I thought he was just kidding. I said, "You don't watch *What's Happening!!*" Then he proceeded to tell me about this scene where I am talking to a girl, and she says, "Hey, Raj, are you a cool guy?" And I say, "You got change for an ice cube?" That's when I realized that he actually did watch the show, because he said the scene verbatim. That was hard to believe — the great Sidney Poitier watched the show! To this day, I'm still amazed by that.

Getting ready for the movie was challenging. It actually interfered with my plans. We were on hiatus from the show for six months, so I was planning to do all the drugs and partying I wanted to. But now I had a role in the movie.

The first day we had to be there at five in the morning, and I had been up half the night getting high. So, I was sitting there that night thinking, *"This is surreal. Sidney Poitier wants me in his movie, and I can't shake this coke. But I'm going. I'm going to shower and put on my face and be there."* And I did. I made it there, with bright eyes and a smiling face. But thank God there wasn't much for me to do that day. I was very out of it. Thankfully, I had coffee to help get me through.

The following days were equally as rough. I was staying up half the night getting high and coming in with low energy. One day Sidney got in my face. He told me he needed more from me. I knew I had to do better. And I wanted to. I owed it to this man that I loved like a father and looked up to as a role model.

Despite my inner struggles, I saw him smile often when I did a scene. The scene that drew the biggest response from him involved a mock interview session. My character was to act as the employer who was interviewing this guy (played by Edward Love) who says he desperately needs a job because his brother is slow and people laugh at him. He tells me that he needs this job to take care of his mama, and then he starts crying. Sidney never said I had to cry in the scene. I just had to be hard on the guy and then go soft on him and tell him that I think he deserves the job. But in the midst of listening to this guy tell me about his brother being slow, something happened, and I started thinking about my sister and how she has always felt inferior. So I identified with the character in that way. At that point, I'm trying not to cry. But, often, when we try not to cry, that makes us want to cry even more. However, I didn't know this at that time, and I broke down and cried. "Yes! Yes! Sidney exclaimed. And he came over and got right in my face and stared at me. Then I knew I had pleased him. That was the money shot. I knew that was God. I had no idea that would happen that day, but I knew I had achieved what I had wanted to do: to make Sidney proud of me.

We had an amazing cast for that movie. And meeting James Earl Jones, who was another one of my idols, was incredible. He told me that he watched the show, and I shared with him how much I admired his work, particularly his Broadway performance in *Of Mice and Men*. He was spectacular in the role of Lenny, and I told him I wished it had been filmed so that all the world could experience his magic. And I meant it. It was one of the best performances I had ever seen.

The premiere was going to be in Hollywood at the Chinese Theater. Sidney wanted me to host the showing and introduce the film. He wasn't going to be able to attend, so he had asked Roscoe Lee Brown to introduce me. I had a house full of people at home on the day of the premiere, and we were getting high and partying. When you're high on drugs, arbitrary thoughts — good, evil, sexual, whatever — will come into your mind and body. I was still convinced that people were trying to kill me. So, I told my brother and my cousin that I needed to get a hotel room so I could avoid being killed, and relax and get ready for the premiere, which was later that night.

I was in this hotel room alone, and I was still doing coke. I'd tell myself, *"Ok. I'm going to stop in an hour because I have to be rested for the premiere."* (more coke) *"OK, I'm gonna stop. OK, I'm gonna do another... Let me see... If I do another... If I get at least three hours of sleep, and then..."* (more coke)... *"If I get two hours of sleep...* (more coke) *"Ok, if I get one hour of sleep"* (more coke)... *"OK, let me just take a shower and take some NoDoz®, then I'll make the premiere."*

So, I showered and put on a nice pair of black slacks and a champagne shirt. I at least looked sober. I could always turn that on when I needed to. I could play the part and appear lucid. And I pulled it off. I felt like a zombie, but I recall saying great things about the film and about Sidney and about being a part of the movie, and encouraging everyone to enjoy it. But I remember almost nothing else about that evening.

I'll never forget the day we were taking photos for the promos of the movie. The guy who was interviewing us was a huge *What's Happening!!* fan. And while Sidney and Bill Cosby were acting legends in their own right, *What's Happening!!* was one of the most popular TV shows during that time, so most of the questions were directed toward me. One of the questions was "How does it feel to be in a big TV show and a new movie?" And I started talking about how I had worked so hard, and I'd come to LA with nothing, and I'd done this and that... And Sidney put his hand on my shoulder, like a father would do to his son, and he said, "But we must not forget those who paved the way." Looking back, I can really appreciate those words. I appreciated them then. But they mean more to me now. Sidney was saying, in so many words, that I was riding on his shoulders. It was the great pioneering actors, like him and Bill, who had paved the way so that I (and other Black actors) may follow. I will, indeed, never forget.

The Malibu experience was a high time in my life — filled with great people, good music, plenty of drugs, food, and alcohol, and lots of good times. Little did I know that things were about to change. It was just a season. Soon the crowds faded, the music stopped, and the thrills were gone. But the drugs and alcohol stayed, and they became constant companions in my life. I was headed in a downward spiral that I could not control. The sweet seduction of the sexy lady was more enticing than ever. I was held tightly in her embrace, and I didn't want to let go. The coke had me on a rapid dissension to nowhere fast — that would ultimately lead me straight into the belly of the beast.

CHAPTER SEVEN

THE BELLY OF THE BEAST

When the show was cancelled, in the spring of '79, that was a dark day. The producers didn't tell us. We went on hiatus after shooting the third season, and we never returned. One day I went to the newsstand to get a paper, and the guy selling the paper told me the show had been cancelled. I went into deep depression for a while after that. I was living alone at the time, so I drank a lot, and I continued to do drugs. It was a way out. I just wanted to escape. I went to the nearest Bristol Farms and bought a bunch of domestic and foreign beers. After a few weeks of that routine, guilt began to overwhelm me, and I stopped drinking and started doing my five prayers a day. Prayer always makes me feel at peace.

I took a shower and put on a white robe. I started reading my Koran, and I began to feel in tune with God. Then I started hearing the voice of Jesus, and that was scary. I didn't want to hear the voice of Jesus. I didn't want to hear any voices. I started drinking to run from it. As the devil would have it, I ran into a friend who had coke, a new kind of coke—freebase.

Freebase and crack cocaine became the preferred drugs during that time. Once again, she seduced me. Freebase is so addictive no one can do it just once and put it down. I don't care how holy you are. Stay in your lane and stay away from the lady in that pipe.

The first hit is beyond ecstasy, and from then on you're chasing that same high, which you will never experience again. I reconnected with my friend Brad. He was an up-and-coming rock star at the time. He was popular with the ladies and had a beautiful girlfriend whom I adored. He had been with Universal, but they cut his group from the label once they changed executive personnel. So both of us were drowning in misery, and freebase seemed like the perfect anecdote.

Brad was a talented and prolific songwriter, and he had an amazing voice. Redd Foxx loved me like a son. He had his own managing company, so I asked him if he would let Brad come by the studio because he needed a deal. Redd told me to bring him by and let his people check him out. I brought him over, and he played some of his music and sang for them. They fell in love with him. But everyone falls in love with Brad. He really is a good person. Before we left, they offered him a deal.

Brad jumped behind the wheel when we got back to the car. He started drinking some Jack Daniels, and was getting beyond drunk. He started driving very fast; the car was swerving more and more by the second. He started looking at me and talking, barely looking at the road at all. He asked, "What do you want? Why are you getting me a deal? What is your story?"

By then he was really scaring me. I believe he felt that no one would do something like that for him without wanting his body or something in return. In Hollywood, there is a lot of casting couch. But that wasn't me. I finally got him to calm down by letting him know that I wasn't expecting anything from him but his friendship.

Brad and I continued to party. One night we met a lady at a party who was a millionaire. Throughout the night, she kept telling us that she was a millionaire. She had a lot of cocaine in aluminum foil, and she shared it with us. We ended up going home with her. When we got to her house, she and Brad went into her bedroom and had sex. I was in the living room enjoying the rest of the coke she had given me, along with a beer. All of a sudden, the front door opened and in walked her husband — a tall, handsome, friendly man. I say friendly because he came in and spoke, with no questions asked, as if something like this had happened before. Brad and the young lady came out, and she and her husband started to argue. Brad and I left. About a year later, Brad married her.

Brad and I continued to hang out together. We really had some good times. Although Brad was an incredible singer, he never gave himself credit. He didn't believe he could make it as a singer. Being actors, we both, of course, loved movies. We critiqued and discussed them at great lengths all the time.

I stayed with him and his new wife from time to time, but I soon got tired of the drugs and freebasing. I began to feel surrounded by darkness. And I knew this was going nowhere. I knew I had to get out of there. So I asked him to take me home. When he refused, I showered and took a sheet off the bed. I went in the living room and wrapped myself in the sheet and started praying. He looked at me and said, "Oh, now you're doing the 'God thing'." I knew I had to get out. I had no peace there.

I went to stay with my sister because I had no income, and I had been evicted from my apartment in. She lived in Hawthorne, California, with her boyfriend at the time. I had never heard of Hawthorne before, but the great thing about living there was that I was near the mosque in Inglewood. So, I could walk there and clear my head and get my thoughts together, get in tune with God, and try to stay away from the drugs. I felt good doing my five prayers a day, especially when I went to the mosque to pray with my other brothers, who I felt were more spiritual than I was.

I had been staying with my sister for about six months when my lawyer called and told me I had a check for $17,000. I was shocked. I couldn't believe it! The show was in syndication somewhere in the Midwest. So I bought my sister and her boyfriend a thousand dollars' worth of groceries, and I bought my niece a bicycle. Then I gave each of them a few hundred dollars. About a month later another check came for $10,000. Then another check came. These checks for thousands of dollars kept coming. All I could think was, "Oh, my God!"

My sister and her boyfriend thought the checks had started rolling in because of my Islamic faith. At first, I was considered a heathen, and I was told I was going to hell for "messing around in that foolishness." But now they were ready to convert to Islam. *Huh??* They told me they were ready to become Muslims. So, we went to the mosque, and they made a declaration of faith. They changed their names to Muslim names. And they even got married, because they were told that they were living in sin.

But as soon as the checks stopped coming in because the IRS came for my taxes, the robes came off, the Muslim names went away, and I was a heathen again! Although I was left with a few hundred dollars, like I said, I was really bad with money. I spent it and gave it away. I helped my brothers at the mosque when they needed help. I would help anyone who needed money. That's the truth. Anyone who knows me knows that. Although I squandered it all, I can take some comfort in knowing that a good portion of it helped others.

One of the best friends God ever gave me was a brother named Yusef. He was very serious about the faith. Because he knew I was trying to stay off the drugs, he told me that I should go to Pakistan. They had a spiritual forty-day program over there, where I could deepen my faith. He said, "You really need to be in a high spiritual program where you can really learn the value of your faith, and it sticks to your heart. Otherwise, you're going to keep going back to the drugs." I decided to heed his advice.

I needed to get a passport. But in order to do that, I needed my birth certificate, which I could not find. I told some of my brothers at the mosque, who happened to be from Pakistan, that I wanted to go but I couldn't find my birth certificate. They told me to pray about finding it. I did. And, sure enough, I found it.

When I was all set to go, I told my brothers that I was worried about my mother. She, of course, is a Christian woman, and I didn't want her to know where I was going and why.

They said, "Look, in Islam, mothers are next to God. So, if your mother doesn't want you to go, you can't go." I said, "What if I tell her I'm going to travel and talk to people about God? I just won't say which God or religion." They thought it was a good idea, so that's what I did. When I called and gave her the news, she said, "Oh, that's so beautiful!"

A few days later, some of my brothers from the mosque and I left for Pakistan. We stayed in a big, beautiful mosque. We did our five prayers a day. It was an awesome experience because the people were very friendly, and there were no drugs or alcohol to resist. There were also no newsstands, televisions, or movies. I was in a total Islamic environment twenty-four/ seven, for forty days.

Our first prayer began at either four or five in the morning. Then there was the noon prayer, followed by another prayer and then two more prayers before bedtime. The morning prayers were the hardest to get up for. But we didn't have to worry about oversleeping. The elder brothers, graced with white beards, came promptly each morning, saying, "Brother, brother. Get up!" And they stood over each of us until we got up. Oh, my Lord! They looked so holy, and they seemed to glide, as if they could float or levitate at any moment.

Then we'd wash up, because we always prepared ourselves to go before the Creator. Our hands and nostrils had to be clean. We had to gargle and rinse our mouths. Our feet and our heads had to be washed. It's all symbolic of going before the Creator in purity. If we urinated, defecated, or passed gas between prayers, we had to wash up all over again.

The group prayer was led by the Imam, which is like a minister or bishop. The Imam leads the prayer, and the others follow. Usually, that Imam has knowledge of the Koran, and he can speak it in Arabic.

Breakfast followed morning prayer. We sat in small groups, with the food placed in the middle of each group. Then everyone would reach in and eat. It was a great thing because eating with a group creates unity and makes you eat less. I loved the camaraderie and sharing. Everyone was more concerned with making sure others were getting enough to eat and were satisfied, which made us feel full sooner. It was a beautiful sight to see.

We had lectures going on all day on various topics. I listened to lectures about patience, serving God, and temperance. But, without fail, the five prayers were going to happen in Pakistan, no matter what was going on. Even the buses and trains stop. At that time, everyone starts washing up and preparing for prayer, and someone's going to lead it. There's always some person on the trains and buses who will lead the prayer, and everyone prays. After prayer, the trains and buses continue on to their destinations, and everyone picks up where they left off.

Our purpose there as Americans was to strengthen our faith and remind the Pakistanis who weren't going to the mosque and were taking their faith for granted to come back and fulfill the obligation to pray and renew their faith. So, we'd knock on doors and say, "As-salāmu □alaykum. I'm from America." They were taken aback by having an African American inviting them to come to the mosque and pray.

One day we went to a university to invite students to the mosque. I remember this well-dressed kid. I could tell he was really smart. He had heard it all before, and I could tell he was bored. He looked at me as if to say, "Hurry up and get it over with." But he listened. I said, "We'd like to invite you to come to the mosque and pray with us." His facial expression said, "Boy, please. I was born Muslim. Step away, newbie." But that was part of the experience.

The communal breakfasts, lunches, and dinners started getting to me because, after all, I am American. I started thinking about all those different hands going in the food, and whether they were really clean. I'm not saying they weren't, but my mind was really reeling over the fact that all those hands were in the food. And the flies. Oh, my God! There were plenty of flies. Everyone was shooing flies off the food, but they kept right on eating. I think the flies really made me sick, literally.

After a couple of days of feeling ill, the brothers took me to a doctor, and I was given some medicine. But what made matters even worse was the fact that I hadn't communicated with my mother at all since I'd been there. I had told certain friends to tell her that I was OK and that I was focusing on God and prayer, so I couldn't talk. I would have nightmares about my mother. In the dreams, she was sick, and I wasn't there. It seemed so real. I know my mother. She has a sixth sense about her children. I could sense that she was concerned about me.

Then I would have sexual dreams. Although I was in a mosque, far and away from any sexual images, my natural male desires began to surface. I told the brothers about the sexual dreams, and they told me I was being attacked by the devil.

They'd say, "He knows how to attack you, and he knows where your weaknesses are. You just have to pray harder and ignore the attacks, and ask God for strength." Those brothers prayed for me, and soon the attacks stopped.

It wasn't until the last week that I finally adjusted to the heat and the food. And I was no longer struggling with sexual desires. There was no temptation at the mosque because the women always prayed in a separate area, behind the men, and the women were always covered. The men were covered, too. They were very strict about that.

One of the most beautiful experiences I had in Pakistan took place during that last week. I heard young Muslims—some as young as nine years old—recite long passages of the Koran verbatim. It was truly amazing.

During the last week, I was beginning to think that maybe I belonged there. There were no temptations—no liquor stores, no drug dealers, no pornography, no body parts revealed. I decided I was going to go home and tell Mom I was a Muslim and that I was moving to Pakistan, but I'd come home several times a year. This was the answer to my prayers. I knew I'd never do freebase cocaine here.

On one of my last days in Pakistan, one of the elder Pakistani brothers stopped me. He said, "Sit with me awhile." Where are you from?" I said, "America." He said, "Where in America?" I said, "California." He asked, "What do you do?" I said, "I'm an actor." He said, "Good actor or bad actor?" I said, "Good actor." Then I said, "I really get it now. This is where I should be. There are so many temptations in America. I really struggled with the temptation of drugs and alcohol. I've been here for almost forty days without the first temptation to do any type of drugs or alcohol. I have made up my mind. I'm going home and talk with my mother." Then he looked at me and said, "No, no, no. That's selfish. That's very selfish. You don't do anyone any good by being a Muslim here. Everyone is Muslim here. There are no challenges. You are not helping to spread the Islamic faith by being here. If you're in America, you're a great example. People will want to be Muslim because they see your example. If you're strong in the midst of those temptations like you are here, then people will see that it is your faith that keeps you from doing all those bad things."

I was really crisp at that point. That was not what I was expecting, nor was it what I wanted to hear. I understood what he was saying. Truth be told, I knew I couldn't live that far away from my mother. My mother and I have always been very close. It would have been very hard for me to be away from her. I'd always be wondering if she was alright. I knew my sister and my brother loved her. I just felt that no one was more concerned about her well being than I was.

When I arrived back in the States, I flew into Chicago. I wanted to tell my mother the truth. In order to get to Gary, Indiana, I had to fly to Chicago and take a bus to Gary. I had my robe and sandals on, and I had a kufi on my shaved head. This is the image my mother saw when she picked me up from the bus station. For the first time, she stared at me in a way that always haunts me still. Although we were, and still are, very close, in that moment I sensed a distance that started to grow between us. And it lasted throughout all the time that she had to cope with me being a Muslim. She looked at me as though she hated me. I really thought my mother hated me. The expression of my new faith frightened and angered her. She didn't know what to make of it. She'd never seen me look that way.

Although it felt like hate to me, it was actually disappointment that my mother felt. But it was still more than I could bear. I tried to explain the religion to her. She asked, "What about Jesus? What do they think about Jesus?" I knew she was not going to like the answer. "Well, they believe he was a prophet, not the Son of God. And he wasn't crucified. As Muslims, we love Jesus. We just don't see him the way you see him. Muslims see Jesus as a great prophet who performed miracles. I'm not going to change, but I'm not anti-Christian. I'm not anti-anything." She was done. "Oh, no. I don't want to hear all that mess," she said. You're going to hell, boy."

Later that night, I lay in bed in the darkness, and I could still see the look in my mother's eyes. I cried myself to sleep because I wasn't going to stop being Muslim. I had made up my mind that I would be a Muslim forever. I felt I was between a rock and a hard place. I wanted my mother to love me and look at me with the unconditional love in her eyes that I had always seen when she looked at me. And I wanted to stay in Islam at the same time. But she wasn't looking at me in that way any longer. Although her look eventually softened, I would still get those disappointed looks occasionally.

I was a little depressed when I left Gary to head back to Los Angeles. I really felt like my mother hated me. She later told me that she never hated me. Because of Jesus, she could never hate. She was just disappointed and even angry at me.

I was still living with my sister, and I continued to do five prayers a day. I was walking to the mosque and trying to stay focused on staying on the right track. I was drinking Yuban coffee. I don't know why. For some reason, I got into the black Yuban coffee with honey. It gave me a lot of energy, and I could walk to the mosque and talk to the brothers.

I don't know what triggered it. It was strange. But one day it just came out of nowhere — that desire for cocaine, weed, and sex. But it was mainly for drugs. I had been clean and sober for over forty days, thinking and believing that I would be that way forever. Although Yusuf was happy that I had gone to Pakistan, he said I probably should have stayed there for four months. I knew that wouldn't have happened. I couldn't be away from my mom that long. He kept saying to me, "Look, my brother. The high you get from the freebase can't compare to the high you get if you just pray to God. If you really get into your faith, God can take you higher than any freebase high can."

My submission to the temptations was gradual. I started drinking beer first. I would go to the store dressed in regular clothes and sneak the bottles home. I would keep them hidden from my sister. I didn't want anyone to know my secret. The dark forces will provide whatever you're looking for. If you're looking for the good things in life, you become a magnet for those things. But, if you're looking for the things that will bring you down and make you depressed and upset, those things will come as well. I wasn't even aware of it, but I had become a magnet for the familiar dark things.

Soon, a friend I used to get high with called me, and the next thing I knew we were getting some coke together. I was in such torment. For forty days, I had experienced heaven on earth, in the sense that I had been in an environment that was free of drugs and full of God's peace. Now, here I was, feeling the guilt and shame of giving in to the very thing I had been running from. I found myself wanting even more freebase to escape the guilt and shame. After coming down from the high, I found the guilt was always there, waiting for me. So, I needed to escape it all over again. It was a vicious cycle.

The body wants to feel good. The body just wants that unnatural high. Really, it's a lie. It's ecstasy you've never felt before, and you want to feel it over and over and over again. But the thing is, it's not natural. So many people OD'd because they just wanted more of the pipe. They kept smoking it, smoking it until their hearts burst. I was blessed because drug dealers always stopped me from OD'ing. Otherwise, I'd be dead. The drug dealers, the pimps, their wives, the prostitutes, and the call girls would look out for me. Whenever I was getting high with anyone, that person would notice that I was getting real feverish to do more and more coke…more coke, more coke. And they would say, "Stop, Ernie, or you're gonna die. You're gonna kill yourself, brother. Your heart can't take that." I knew then to allow myself to come down and feel the depression. I had to accept that I'd get depressed when my high was leaving. I had to wait and then go back up again. So, I learned.

When I was getting high, I would watch TV to keep my mind focused. The other users would start getting paranoid and look out the window and under the couch, and I didn't do all that. I remember one drug dealer saying to me, "You're the strongest nigga I've ever seen. Uh-huh, I see you. There's a lot going on. You're sitting there taking all this freebase and Remy Martin and weed, and you're not budging. You ain't walking around, and you ain't doing a whole lot of talking." I had learned to discipline myself. Ironically, I really believe my religious upbringing had a lot to do with that. That's the truth. If that foundation hadn't been there, there was no way, with the amount of drugs and the strange people around me, that I would have survived. The people around me weren't like people I knew or had grown up with. They could have killed me or allowed me to OD. But God's grace and mercy were surrounding me, even then. Yet, I often felt that God hated me. I would talk to God and say, "Don't let me die, Lord. Keep me, Lord. Lord, I'm playing hooky because I'm in so much pain. You know the show was canceled. I don't have any money. Lord, I just want to feel good."

When the coke was gone, I'd go home and smoke marijuana. Usually, the marijuana and liquor would knock me out because I'd been up all day. But if they didn't, I'd take sleeping pills. Anything was better than feeling the guilt and the disappointment.

I eventually convinced myself into believing that I was disciplined with my habit, which was dumb. Anytime you hear somebody say, "I freebase, but I've got a handle on it. I balance it out. I freebase once a month," don't believe it. There's no such thing. But I decided I was going to buy some coke and ration it out. So, I gave it to my friend David. I said, "Look, we did this much. Take the rest and don't give it to me—no matter what I say or how much I beg for it. I want you to hold on to it." Then we went to a restaurant to eat. As we were leaving the restaurant, I said, "Hey, man. Forget about what I said. I'ma need that. I need a hit." Of course, he said no. I said, "Man, give me my sh*t." And he still refused. Well, by this time I was cussing and threatening to kick his ass. He said, "No, Ernie. You told me not to give it to you, no matter what. Look, man. I'm not going to do it." He turned and started to walk away. I started shouting right there on Sunset Boulevard. "Give me my sh*t! Give me my sh*t, man!" I took off my cowboy boots and threw them at him. He looked at me as if I had lost my mind and said, "You see people looking at you? You're a celebrity, you idiot!" I didn't care about any of that. I just wanted my coke. That's when he said, "Take this sh*t, man. But give me some of it, too." There we were, in the seductive hands of the lady — the hot, hot lady.

I had been staying at the YMCA since I had started using drugs again and the residuals had stopped coming in. David was my roommate. He was an actor as well, and he had fallen on hard times. One day David and I were talking with a drug dealer, and the dealer told me that I needed to meet Muhammad Ali. That stuck with me. I believe in visualizations. So, I got magazines with pictures of Ali in them. I would pray and tell God, "I want to meet Muhammad Ali." But, because I was in awe of him, I didn't visualize meeting him right away. I visualized meeting Kool & the Gang first. I knew they were Muslims, too. I got photos of them, and I would stare at the photos and pray. One fine day in the summer of '82, David looked out the window and said, "Ernie, there's a big limousine outside."

Out of that limo stepped Kool & the Gang, no lie! David called me a warlock. That was the first time he'd said that. They came to play basketball at the YMCA. I went down to the gym to meet them. They were all fans of the show, and to me, they were one of the best groups in the world. I found a moment to approach the lead singer, J.T. Taylor, one of the best voices ever. I almost asked for help, but then I totally froze and started being a fan again.

Then I decided to focus on Ali. A week later, David wanted to go to Hollywood and just hang out. While riding around, we ended up on a side street, and a lady came up to us and said, "Hey, Muhammad Ali is at the Magic Shop doing magic tricks. The store looks closed, but it's not. Just open the gate and go on in." She just walked right up to the car and told us that Ali was there. My friend said, "I know you're a damn warlock now. You're definitely a warlock." I said, "Man, that's just prayer." I really did pray. I had been looking at the pictures, but praying to God made it a reality.

When we walked in, people immediately asked me for my autograph. While I was signing autographs, I felt this pull. Ali had a strong and stern stare. After signing autographs for a while, I'd had enough, and I said, "I'm here to see Muhammad Ali, y'all. I love you, but we're here to see the champ, right?" And I went over to Ali, and he said, "Roger! Roger! Do that laugh!" And I did. Then I said, "But you don't watch our show. You don't watch *What's Happening!!*" He said, "Yes, I do. Do it again! Do it again!" And he started laughing. He didn't laugh out loud. His mouth was open but there was no sound coming out. But he was cracking up. That was a moment I'll never forget. He said, "You need anything?" I said, "I need your autograph!" He looked at me as if to say, "Yeah, right." Then he said,

"Well, here's my number, in case you do need something." He read me. He saw right through me. I took the autograph, and I thanked him. He said, "Call me if you need anything."

It took me three months to call him. My pride was in the way. Pride is a dangerous thing. When God offers to bless us through people, we shouldn't hide from it or delay it. It's all God. It doesn't matter who it is. Receive it. We're worthy of it because we're called the righteousness of God. If you believe in Christ, you're called the righteousness of God. So, you're supposed to be blessed.

As I was going up the steps to Ali's mansion, my legs got weak. I had never had that feeling before. That was scary. When I saw him, he had a big o' smile on his face. He was so happy to see me. He couldn't have been friendlier. He said, "You're not a bum. Don't feel bad. I needed help. Joe Frazier helped me. It's no big thing about me helping you, OK? Don't be in awe of me. I'm just a nigga trying to get bigger." But I was in awe. It took a while. It took a good year for me to just calm down and treat him as a friend.

He set me up in a hotel. It was a kitchenette hotel on Vine Street. I told him I needed laser surgery for my eye. He said, "OK, I'll take care of that. I'm going to give you money to put in your pocket, too." As good as he was being to me, I still opened my mouth and said something really stupid. I was standing there with my suit on, staring out the window in his office, and I said, "You know, Ali, it's really not your money. It's God's money." It seemed like everyone in that room wanted to punch me in my mouth, including David. He looked at me as if to say, *"What is wrong with you?"*

Ali looked at me and said, "Yeah, and God uses men to do His work. And you're supposed to thank that bridge that God uses to bless you." Then I realized I still had my nose up in the air. "Yes, you're right about that. You're right, Ali. And I thank you." Then the nose came down, and humility started to set in. It was a struggle. And he knew it was pride. I really was in awe, and I was very happy. I just didn't want to show it.

Ali took care of my surgery, and was always offering to help me. He told me I could visit anytime, just call ahead and let him know. The first time I came by, he knew I wouldn't ask for money. He was in his office with friends. He excused himself and came out into the hall to speak to me: "You need anything?" I said, "Hmm, you know," while shrugging my shoulders. So, he pulled out some cash and gave it to me. I will never forget how he'd just pull out hundreds of dollars and started peeling them off slowly, one by one. Then he'd say, "Let me know when to stop." That's the kind of heart he had.

Money and fame meant nothing to him. He often said God gave him boxing so that he could have a platform where he could help everyone and be a source of peace. During the Iraqi war, when Saddam Hussein took the hostages, Ali went over there and got some of the hostages and brought them back. He had that type of power. He gave to Jewish senior citizens. He gave land to Christians so they could build schools. He gave to everybody. He was ALL about faith. He was proud of being Muslim, but he helped anyone. He never attacked anyone's faith. And everyone, from all religions, loved him. If he went to a city where well-known evangelists or preachers were, they would come and see him in his hotel suite. They would have their Bibles and he would have the Koran, and they would have discussions. And he'd always let them end the meeting with a prayer in Jesus' name.

I was in the kitchenette for a while. I would go to the mosque with Ali. I was trying to steer clear of the drugs, but even in the midst of a higher class of people, the drugs were there. The dealers called me "Roger Dodger" because I would try to avoid them. Again, pimps and prostitutes have always been my biggest fans, but Ali had gotten me in this kitchenette, and I knew I couldn't hang around that type of crowd. But one day, one of the pimps said, "Hey, Roger Dodger. Man, we ain't gonna hurt you. We love you, man. We watch you on TV every day." So, I finally went over and started talking to them. And I was back to hitting the pipe again.

A few days later, I was sitting and talking with Ali. He said, "I found you out! I found you out! You've been hanging in those streets. You're doing them drugs. I'm done with you. I'm through. You ain't getting nothing else." I smiled at him. My acting skills kicked in. I gave him a big o' smile, as if I didn't know what he was talking about. I said, "Ali, I don't know. If I were you, I'd be done with me, too, if you believe those lies." His look was full of anger. He said, "I know you're lying." I said, "So, if you believe that, Ali, I wouldn't give me another dime if I were you. I'm gonna speak well of you because you've gone well beyond the call of duty." And I walked right out of the mansion.

Of course, Ali continued to help me. He did not cut me off like he said he would because his heart was too big. He was a god-send, a lifesaver. Truth be told, I would have been on the street if it wasn't for him.

As time went on, Ali and I became very close friends. I met his kids and discovered that they were huge fans. They would stay with Ali every summer. They loved me, and I loved them. Their love and admiration came at a time when I really needed it. I am forever grateful for the love and support I received from Ali and his family. He was truly a blessing, and I miss him dearly.

A little while later, he tried to help me with a show I had written called *Millie's Place*. I asked Sony Television if they would be interested if Ali funded it. They said they would be interested in producing it as a pilot if Ali would put up the money. Of course, they couldn't promise that it would be a hit or that it would even be aired. But I had to take a chance. Unfortunately, the negotiations fell through, but Ali did try.

After the negotiations for *Millie's Place* fell through, I told Ali that I wanted to present another *What's Happening!!* to Sony Television. I was amazed at how popular the show still was and at the amount of fans who still showed me so much love wherever I went. But I couldn't get an appointment with the executives at Sony. Ali said, "Well, why can't you get an appointment?" I said, "Well I just don't think they will want to talk about a new *What's Happening!!* show." He said, "There are no rules. Go! As long as you're not hurting anybody, just go." It was Ali who gave me the courage. He gave me the determination to reach beyond the "no." Sometimes there may be obstacles in our way, but we still have to press on. The road to our destiny may not always be easy, but God will give us the strength and determination to move on. If he is for us, no one can stand against us. And no weapon can defeat us. When we trust him and ask for his guidance, his favor will precede us, and he will work on our behalf.

I decided to take Ali's advice. I didn't know what was going to happen, but I knew I had to trust God and see where this would lead. I wanted desperately to be free of the darkness in the belly of the beast, and I believed this would be the avenue that would lead me out of there.

CHAPTER EIGHT

BORN AGAIN

After Ali had given me the confidence to move forward, I took my treatment of the new *What's Happening* to Sony Pictures. I don't know why I didn't wear a suit, but I dressed in jeans and a T-shirt to make my pitch for my future. The security guard recognized me and asked me who I was there to see. I told him I was there to see Herman Rush. He said, "OK, go right on in." I was surprised because he didn't even look at the list to see if I had an appointment. I thought, "*Oh, my God. Ali had said it! He was right. There are no rules.*"

When I got to Sony Pictures, I was greeted by the secretary. She was so kind. She said, "Hi, Ernest. Do you have an appointment?" I said "No, I don't, but I have a new *What's Happening!!*, and I want to talk with Herman about it." She said, "OK. Well, sit down and hold on a minute." While I was sitting there, Herman happened to be walk by. He looked at me and immediately said, "Hi Ernest. You need something?" I said, "Oh, yeah. I'm here to talk with you about bringing *What's Happening!!* back. I have a new treatment on the show." He said,

"OK. Well, leave it here." I was thankful because he was very gracious, considering that I didn't have an appointment. I gave the treatment to the secretary and was about to leave when she said, "No. Write a letter from your heart stating why you think there should be another *What's Happening!!*" So, I did.

In the letter, I mentioned being mobbed at Disneyland, Knott's Berry Farm, and Magic Mountain. I also mentioned that I was down to my last million (ha, ha, ha). I went on to say that Clint Eastwood and Steven Spielberg were trying to give me deals, but I didn't want any of them. I just wanted a new *What's Happening!!*

And then I waited. I had a really good feeling about it. Several days later, I got a letter from Herman saying, "Thank you for your enthusiasm, but there's not an audience for a new *What's Happening!!*" I was hurt and a little disappointed, but I was not about to give up. I said, "*I'm right, God. You wouldn't let me feel this if it wasn't true.*" Not only did I feel it, I had experienced being mobbed by crowds — literally, that's what happened.

I had recently attended a Sister Sledge concert, and the sisters couldn't even perform because the fans kept screaming at them to let them know I was there. The sisters had to acknowledge me before they could continue with their concert. So, that letter did not reflect reality. It was not only I who had enthusiasm, but many others did, too.

From that point, I started a letter-writing campaign. I went to Gary, Indiana, first to meet with the mayor because I had made a lot of appearances for him during his campaign for re-election. I said, "Mayor, you owe me." And he said, "No problem." He called a press conference and said his signature would be the first on the national signature campaign to bring *What's Happening!!* back.

My agent and manager both left me. So, I got a new manager, and she connected me with Green Vine Agency. They were beautiful, such sweethearts. They were some of the top agents at the time, and they had taught a lot of people in the business. They couldn't have been kinder or more encouraging. They said, "OK. We believe you." They bought into the dream.

Months went by, and I was still busy with the signature campaign. Ali suggested that I start becoming active in the community and start giving back. So I went to Compton and started an acting workshop. We had a lot of fun with the kids and adults. Some of the best people in the world live in Compton, California. One day I stopped by my usual spot to each lunch, a sandwich shop that was owned by a friend of Ali's — Akil Salaam. He and his children had been a true blessing to me. While eating at his shop, I got a call from my agent. She said, "Ernest, are you sitting down?" I said, "No." She said, "You need to sit down. They're bringing *What's Happening!!* back." I could have fainted right there. I felt weak in the knees, just like I had when I was walking up those steps to meet Ali. I told Akil and his kids as soon as I got off the phone. They were so happy and excited. I told Akil that I wanted him to be my bodyguard. I wanted to give him a job because I had gotten the call while I was in his shop. And he happily accepted.

Then I called Fred to give him the news, but he had already heard. He said, "Ernie Bern! We can't mess up this time, Ernie Bern. Uh-uh." I said, "You're right, Fred." He said, "Ernie

Bern, we gotta do exactly as they tell us. We gotta cooperate because God gave us another opportunity. This is a blessing from God. Ernie Bern, let's pray. I'ma pray in the name of Jesus, and you pray in the name of Allah." And we did.

Initially, they only wanted me for seven episodes. I was confused and hurt by this, since I was the main character in the show. I told Ali about it, and I told him that they wanted to meet with me. He handed me a note and said, "Well, give them this message when you meet with them."

So, I gave them the message. It said, "Rivers, ponds, lakes, and streams—they all have different names, but all contain water, and they all beautiful. So are the religions. They have different names, but all contain truth, and they are beautiful. Don't mess with my boy." They asked, "What does he mean by that?" I said, "I don't know. He told me to hand it to you." They said, "We love you, man. We want you in every episode."

It was good seeing the cast again. We all just fell into place and got to work. We had the table read on Monday, and on Thursday we did the run-through for the producers and the network. Everything had been wonderful up to the day of filming, which was always on Friday. Now, this is seven years later—1985. *What's Happening Now!!* is a miracle because people said it would never happen. And all of a sudden, my voice was gone! I couldn't speak. I don't know why. I couldn't say a word the day of the taping. I had been waiting for this day for seven years, and not a word was coming out of my mouth.

They took me to the top doctors in Glendale because the show was being shot at Glendale Studios, which was run by a great guy, Al Makhanian, and his brothers. The doctors said there was nothing wrong with me. It was all psychosomatic.

Now the producers were getting upset, and the cast members were looking at me cross-eyed. So, Akil called Ali and said, "Ali, you gotta get down here." I don't know why he called Ali, but he did. Then he said, "I called Ali. He's coming. He's a little tired. He was overseas, but he's coming to see you." Akil knew that, if Ali came, my voice would come back. But there was a part of me that was wondering what would happen if it didn't. I was really in turmoil. This was important, and each episode cost over $200,000. A lot of money was on the line.

When Ali arrived, the producers were like little children. "What do you need, Ali?" They ordered staff, "Go and get more of this, and put some food there." Ali didn't want any of that. He was focused on me. He wanted me to know that everything was going to be alright. And you know what? Because he was there, my voice came back. That was our first show. The rest is history!

While I was going through the strange predicament with my voice, Mindy Cohn, one of the stars from *The Facts of Life*, stopped by the set. She gave me words of encouragement, in hopes of my voice returning. She was a big fan and a god-send. Her thoughtfulness will never be forgotten.

There's an old saying that goes, "Prayer changes things." But some things — and people — never change. Once again, Fred somehow came to believe that he was the star of the show. There was mutiny on the set. My friend Fred, who had prayed with me in the name of Jesus, while applying and pleading the blood of Jesus, was now telling me, "Ernie Bern, the truth is, I am the star of the show. It's just a fact." I knew the drugs were influencing him. So, I couldn't reason with him. He said, "Just face the fact that I'm the star, and you're not. Without me there is no show." He wanted a million dollars, and he was not returning to the show without it. The first season had been great. We all had gotten along beautifully. But, unfortunately, it didn't last.

Soon it became big news, featured on *Entertainment Tonight:* "Fred Berry wants his MDD, Million Dollar Deal." The producers wanted me to reason with him. They were asking everybody to reason with him, but there was no getting through to him.

And that's how Martin Lawrence came on board. Truth be told, Martin became a superstar because of his TV show, *Martin,* which is one of my all-time favorite sitcoms. But Martin's first television character was Maurice on *What's Happening Now.* So, Martin was in, and Fred was out.

Around that time, we had a record deal with MCA Records to record a song called *What's Happening Now.* It was originally supposed to be Fred, Haywood, and me on the track, but Fred pulled out. He said God had told him that I was going to keep all the money. So, he didn't want to be a part of it. That's when Danielle became a part of the contract. Danielle, Haywood, and I completed the project. We performed the song in San Diego for thousands of kids.

Along with Martin Lawrence, the producers added another talented young man, Ken Sagoes, to the show. They were buddies on the show, and even off the set they were friends. Their characters worked in the soda shop. During that time, the show was coming to an end. But, instead of the two years it had initially been slated for, the show lasted three years. So that was a huge blessing. I thank God for Herman Rush.

By this time, I had gotten engaged to a beautiful young lady, Mecca. She was a beautiful Muslim school teacher and the mother of two great kids. She and I got along in every way. We didn't have sex because we were always chaperoned. But we talked about it because, in Islam, we talked about everything. There is a contract, which allows each party to say what he or she wants and doesn't want. We were very attracted to each other. But, as I said, there was always a chaperone. But one night we went out to a movie on our own and came back to her place. While standing there in her living room, we could feel the physical attraction between us grow more intense. I was encouraged by our chemistry.

She was such a sweetheart and a good woman. When I went back on the cocaine, I remember calling her and crying, "I don't want to be back on coke. I have the show now, and I need to be sober." She said, "Don't worry. I'm coming over there." And she came. She asked me when the next meeting for cocaine anonymous would be held, and she took me there.

I initially thought I was going to marry Mecca, but if I was being truly honest with myself, I knew deep inside I couldn't do it. I didn't have the nerve to tell Mecca straight out, so I created an argument to give us an excuse to end it.

I got engaged a second time, to a young lady named Skye, a highly spiritual lady who was a few years older than I was. What I loved about her was her strength. I remember an associate of mine telling Skye that he had power to put hexes and spells on people. She told him, "Before the words reach your lips, they're already done to you." I never forgot that, and I've said that many times to people who claimed to be witches and practiced voodoo. Skye was also a vegetarian. I tried to be one while we were engaged, but I had to have some hamburgers and barbecue ribs in my life. We broke up, but we remained friends. She's an awesome human being.

Looking back now, I've come to realize that I'm not the marrying kind. It wasn't about being a provider or being faithful. I had no problem being a giving and faithful man. But the thought of being tied and accountable to one person for the rest of my life was more than I could bear, and I just couldn't do it. I had tried to go through the motions to please everyone else. I thought that's what they wanted for me. But that's not what I wanted.

When *What's Happening Now!!* ended in 1988, I surrendered to the coke again. It got really bad. In hindsight, I realize that God had given me both shows. And I praised him for both of them. But I had made the shows my gods. And when the shows ended, my gods had failed me. Instead of looking to God for the next move in my life, I relied on the drugs to replace the void that the cancellations had created. The coke wooed me and comforted me. So I started going back to the things that made me feel good because I didn't like being depressed. I loved acting, and without the shows or any other acting jobs I felt I had nothing.

Fred had betrayed his prayer, and now I had betrayed mine. In the name of Allah, I had said I would cooperate. I felt I had let God down again. But I was empty without the stage. I was born to entertain. Acting was my craft, my art, my passion.

I felt that nothing else could fill that void, but the drugs helped me cope until the void could be filled.

A few months after the show was cancelled, my agents and my manager suggested that I do stand-up. Stand-up was huge in the '80s, and I was a huge fan of many stand-up comics. I would go to the Comedy Club all the time. I saw Jim Carrey do his first show; he did many amazing impersonations. Sam Kinison was the doorman at that time. Of course, he soon became huge in stand-up. And Andrew Dice Clay was a great comic as well. Sam and Andrew both came on stage late at night when the place was about to close because the club owner knew people would leave. The people hadn't caught on yet. But I really enjoyed them. I thought they were both geniuses. They loved *What's Happening!!* and were huge fans. We'd hang out after leaving the Comedy Club, often going out for hamburgers. They were really nice guys and a lot of fun to hang out with.

I miss Sam a lot. He made me laugh at things I shouldn't have, but Sam made it OK. He was a true genius in my eyes. I was angry at him for dying. I know that sounds stupid, but it's true. He was a great guy.

My agent kept urging me to do stand-up because I had a name. People knew me. Yes, I was funny in the sitcom because I'm an actor — that's my foundation. I could act like a stand-up comedian, but I wasn't really a stand-up comedian. As an actor, I treated it as my new role. I was going to play a stand-up comic.

Robin Harris gave me what I needed. I told him that I needed some material. He said, "You got a tape recorder?" I actually did because I had been practicing some material I already had. What Robin gave me was great, and I felt I had a good fifteen to twenty minutes. But that wasn't enough because, as a celebrity, I needed to have an hour. Most places expected that. I became a regular at the Comedy Store, and I was comfortable for about a good fifteen minutes. After that, I was done.

I decided to take my show on the road. My first show was at a comedy club in Boston. When I got there, I was informed that I was supposed to perform for an hour. Now, this was on a weekend, so I couldn't reach my agent. I knew I had to come up with something. I only had a whopping fifteen minutes of material. So, I left the club and went to a local novelty store and grabbed a tape recorder and a *Rolling On The River* cassette. I had a Tina Turner wig. I was going to start dancing like Tina Turner. I was planning to extend my act by doing silly, random acts.

When I got up and did my first fifteen minutes, everything was going well. Oh, but when those first fifteen minutes were over, I bombed, and you could hear a pin drop. One guy shouted out "Be funny" (or something like that). And I said, "M**f**r, who do you think you're talking to!" The silence was deafening. It was an all-White audience. There was not a Black person in the place. And I knew I had to get off the stage because I was getting ready to go postal on this guy.

But that really scared me because that was so out of my character. Yet, in that moment, I was another person. I was still doing coke, and I was trying to make and defend my reputation and name. I picked up my bag of gimmicks, my tape recorder, and my Tina Turner wig, and I went back to my hotel room.

Leaving that stage in defeat was humiliating and the walk to my hotel seemed to take forever.

The next morning, the agency called me back. They had gotten the message I had left on their machine. They told me that the agreement was for twenty minutes and that the owner was just trying to get more out of me. Now I was really angry. I got on the air at a local Black radio station and told the audience that I needed their help. I felt outnumbered, and I needed some support. So I told them I would love to see them at the club. And that was all it took.

When I arrived at the club that night, there were Black people lined around the block. The owner was livid. My agent and manager called me. My manger said, "Ernie, what did you do? Did you call for Black people to come to the place?" I said, "I sure did." She said, "Well, the owner's upset because the regular customers are going to feel uncomfortable. It's not him. It's his customers." I said, "Look, it's too late. They're out there now. There's nothing I can do about it." I stood there beaming, with a huge smile on my face. It was going to be a good night.

It was a good show, and it was my last. I did my twenty minutes and then I said, "You know what? I hear a lot of negative stuff about Boston being racist. But I'm looking out there at all of you — Black and White sitting together — and I know that's not true. It's such a beautiful sight to see. God bless you. Give yourselves a big round of applause!" The owner was giving me the evil eye. If looks could kill, I would have been dead! That was the beginning and the end of my standup run in Boston and elsewhere.

After returning to LA, I started receiving phone calls from this young guy named Francesco I had met while I was in Boston. He worked at the hotel as a night clerk. We had spoken briefly, and he seemed like a really nice kid. The first time he called me, he immediately apologized because I had not given him my number. He had gotten it from the hotel records. He said, "I could be fired for calling you, Mr. Thomas. But please give me a moment. I'm a super talented rapper; all I need is a chance." And I thought, *"Yeah, he's a lot like me. That is something I would do."* You have to be bold. So I told him to get back with me.

I had gotten back into my usual routine with the drugs, so I was annoyed with this kid because he kept calling me and asking me to help him. He really wanted me to be his mentor and manager. He was constantly leaving messages on my machine and sending me a bunch of letters and photos. But I was hesitant about contacting him because I knew helping him would mean having less time to freebase. One day I was complaining about him to my mom, and she said, "This could be your blessing." What my mother said made sense. Helping him could be a way for me to break away from the drugs.

So I went to New York. Francesco had offered to let me stay with him and his mother in Albany. At that point, I was drinking vodka at eight in the morning, and I was still smoking weed, but I had decided that I wasn't going to do coke anymore. One morning I was sitting and drinking my vodka, and Francesco drank some because he thought it was water. He asked, "Why are you doing that? I thought you said if we have God, we don't need to get high." And I said, "You mind your own business. I'm managing you; you're not managing me." Although I knew he was right, I was not able to stop. So I made sure I was drinking and smoking only when he was not around. I didn't want to be a bad influence on him. But deep inside I knew I needed to get myself together.

A few days later, I was on my way to the village to do standup at one of the clubs. I had been drinking a lot, and I was extremely high because I was really hurting. This was not something I wanted to do. This wasn't me. And I know I wasn't pleasing God. So I was standing in the village, high and feeling sorry for myself while holding back the tears. I felt like I was losing my mind. And I decided right at that moment that I wasn't going to go.

Francesco and I had moved in with a friend in Manhattan to be close to the recording studios. So I got on the subway and went home. When I got to the apartment, no one was there. And that's when I just broke down and cried. I cried out to God. *"Lord, I just don't want to do this anymore – the drugs, the alcohol. And yet, even as I ask you to take this from me, part of me wants some. But I'm asking you to take the desire away, and I can't help you at all. All I'm doing is asking, but I can't help you, because as I'm speaking to you, part of my flesh is yearning for it.*

And I just lay there, and I cried.

I tell people I am indeed a walking miracle. The next day, it was gone. I had no desire for drugs or alcohol. A week went by, a month went by, a year—and still no desire. In social settings, I'd tell people how God delivered me, and they'd say, "Oh, I don't want to drink or smoke around you," and I'd say,

"Oh, that doesn't bother me." I don't attribute it to any religion or regimen. It was all God.

During that time, I was still going to the mosque and secretly going to church. About a month after my rebirth, I met this young man from Nigeria. He was a fan, so we started talking. I started telling him how God had taken away all those desires, and how I felt like I was in another world. I felt in tune with God, and I just wanted love for everybody. And he invited me to a Sufi service. I had heard of Sufism and had read about it briefly when I first became a Muslim. But I didn't know they had actual places of worship.

The Sufis are ostracized by most mainstream Muslims because Sufis include everybody. They embrace all thoughts and approaches to God, and to my surprise, they had books on Christ. They had the Bible and many other books on different religions.

Their services were unlike any I'd ever attended before. There was a lot of meditation. After the service I met the master — a humble man with a kind and godly spirit. When I attended the services I learned so much, and I felt so much peace.

When I told some of my Muslim brothers about it, they looked at me like I was crazy. They thought it was heresy. I was dating a Muslim lady at that time, and when I told her about it, her whole demeanor changed toward me. These were definitely not the reactions I was expecting. When we talk about coming together in love, no one seems to want to hear it, and surely not truly act upon it. So, I went back to the master and shared my experiences with him, and he basically told me that most people have tunnel vision when it comes to spirituality, and they choose to stay right there.

I was still visiting churches, and I started reading my Bible again. And although I wasn't sharing it with anyone, that's where I felt safest, that's where I felt at home. Although others chastised me for my decision to attend the Sufi services, I felt like Sufism gave me the freedom to free my mind and feed my spirit and find my way to where I needed to be—back in church.

A few months later, I discovered that they were holding auditions for *Malcolm X*. I hadn't thought about auditioning, but Francesco was telling me I should go up for it. I knew it would be a long shot, but I got my agent to submit me for an audition. They called me and said, "Ernie, we tried for two weeks. They're not interested. They said they respect you as a comedian, but this is a serious movie." And I thought, Wow. Despite my education and experience at the Academy, I still found myself typecast by Hollywood. Yet, I was determined not to allow that to be my story.

So I contacted my friend David, my old roommate from the YMCA, and asked him if he'd act as my manager and go with me to get my audition. He agreed, and he was awesome. He's always been an amazing actor, very talented. So this was right up his alley. He called and convinced them to give me a five-minute interview, out of respect for my notoriety as a TV icon and my popularity, especially within the Black community. It wasn't an audition, and they weren't obligated to do anything except a courtesy interview.

So I went there with a beautiful expensive pea green suit on that I'd borrowed. I had shined my shoes so shiny they were like mirrors. I had the hair cut and the bow tie. I was going as the character. When I got on the subway, I was in character mode. But I needed to know if I was ready. And while I was sitting there, a White guy was standing across from me, holding on to the overhead strap and drinking from his brown paper bag, staring at me. And, finally he said, in a slurred drunken manner, "I…I …I love Farra CAN." I just looked at him. I didn't even respond. But I was grateful to God for giving me that sign. After the audition, they called me back and said Spike wanted to see me on camera. So I came back and they filmed the scene.

When I came back the third time, the room was filled with the usual actors Spike works with, and I thought to myself, *"Oh, I get it. He's letting me down easy. But at least he was nice about it and gave me a chance."* But I went along with it. That day I did a scene with Denzel. And as we were doing the lines, I really felt comfortable enough to ad lib a bit and really feel the scene. I don't know about Denzel, but I really felt that the chemistry was there. He made it easy, and it felt right.

After the scene, Spike thanked me, so I headed out the room and toward the elevator. Just as I was about to push the button, Spike called me back in the room. I thought, *"OK. Here it comes – the easy letdown."* I was ready. Then he said, "You got the part." Oh! What! I grabbed Spike. I grabbed Denzel. I grabbed everybody in that room! I ran to the elevator, and I ran to the subway. All the while, I was thanking God: *"Oh, my God! I can't believe I got the part! Thank you, God!"* And then it set in:

"Wait a minute; you got a role in Malcolm X. Oh, God! You gotta be good, real good.

I got physically ill four days before we were to start shooting the movie. I used to always get ill right before I was about to start a new role. It was all psychological. I had to give myself the talk. I said, *"OK you gave me this, Lord. I can do this."* And from the first scene, I was all in. I tell people it was like an out-of-body experience for me. It is surreal to me still. That was the movie everybody was trying to get into.

Spike trusted me with scenes that had no lines in it. He told me to ad lib in those places, and if he liked it, he'd keep it. And there were several instances where I had to draw on my creativity and God's anointing, and he kept it in. Watching Denzel become Malcolm was incredible. God has truly blessed Denzel to become one of the best actors of all time. I remember him saying perfection is boring. You don't have to do the same thing in a scene over and over again. Let it be real in the moment. He is truly a legend in his own right.

The premiere was one of the biggest nights in Hollywood. They had to turn many superstars away because there simply weren't enough seats. Everyone wanted to see the movie. It was a huge success, and I felt truly blessed and fortunate to be a part of such an amazing project. To me, it was truly a miracle.

CHAPTER NINE

MIRACLES STILL HAPPEN

In 1993, I was about to move back to Los Angeles to live with my friend Inez Shahid. She had been telling me that I needed to move back so that I could focus on my career and get more accomplished, and I agreed. But it was also during this time that I got a call about my brother. He was in a coma.

Anton has always been more like a son to me than a brother. He was such a beautiful child. I remember the day he came home. He was born on Thanksgiving Day in 1960. Everybody in the neighborhood who knew my mother came over to see the baby. They all had the same perplexed look on their faces when they saw him because he looked like a White child, with blondish fine hairs on his temples and a head full of reddish brown hair. In our community, a light-skinned baby, back in those days, was like the Messiah — viewed as the chosen one.

My sister and I noticed the difference in the way the neighbors treated us. They doted on him constantly. But I loved him, and I spoiled him rotten. We all did. He was like my little toy. I was eleven when he was born, and he always clung to me—even more than he did to our mother. He wanted me to hold him more than anyone else.

At nine years old, he was in a talent contest in Gary, Indiana, at Roosevelt High School. The Jackson 5, Deniece Williams, and many other local kids were also in the contest. My brother was in the dancing competition. The Jackson 5 and Deniece Williams were in the singing category. It was a big talent competition. Diana Ross was there, along with the mayor, who accompanied her. When my mom told me about the competition, I was surprised. I had no idea my brother could dance. She told me that my cousin Liz had been teaching him. So I came home from ISU to see my brother do his thing.

I had never seen my brother dance before, and I didn't want to be embarrassed if he wasn't good. So I came in a little after the competition had started and sat in the back of the auditorium. He was part of a dance group, and they were introduced as Tony and The Black Pearls. And oh, my God! That little kid was doing splits and all sorts of complex moves. He was so confident and strong. The audience was going wild. I sat there in amazement. *What is going on, Lord? Where did he get that from?* I knew this was the gift God had blessed him with, but I was really surprised.

Anton and his group won the dance competition and the Jackson 5 won in the singing category. Deniece came in second or third. I think she came in third, but I can't remember. The entire show was fantastic, such amazing talent, all on one stage.

So, I treated my brother to a trip to New York—to the Apollo Theater. We stayed at the Travelodge because the Travelodge gave credit cards to students. That was our first time in New

York. Our main focus was the Apollo, but we also went to the movies and walked around Central Park. We stayed for three days. When the third day came, Anton's mood had changed. He was sad because he didn't want to leave. He thought the world of our mother and grandmother, but he didn't want to go back home. He said, "I don't want to go back. I love it here." I understood. New York can do that to a person. It really can. I love it, too. But I knew we had to go home. Anton left kicking and screaming. I had to actually pull him every step of the way. I said, "Tony, please. I treated you to a fun trip, but it's over. You know mom and grandma are going to kill me if I return without you. It's never going to happen. If I decided to do that, they'd think I lost my mind. At least go home and tell them that you plan to live here one day. Just work at it, and you'll be back in New York soon." But he was not happy on that trip back home. I was shocked at how he'd fallen in love with the city like that so quickly. Those memories came flooding back to me as I tried to process the news about my brother.

One of the doctors had called to talk to me about my brother's condition. She told me that she'd seen cases like my brother's before. I'll never forget the words she said next as long as I live. "Mr. Thomas, death is hard to get used to, but it's a part of life, and your brother is going to die." She told me that we shouldn't keep him on the life support machine because, if he had a heart attack or his heart failed and they had to revive him, they'd have to break his rib cage and the bones in his chest. She wanted me to know that the process would be gruesome and not worth it to revive him. The doctor told me that the heart attack would be inevitable, and when it did happen, we should let him go. The doctors had seen it many times before. And I hadn't. I didn't want him to suffer. Mom didn't want to make the decision. She had asked the doctors to call me. She wanted me to make the decision.

My cousin Jean was at the hospital. She called me and said, "Ernie, you can't play God. We don't know. What if he lives? What if God works a miracle? Let God have the final say." I had the professionals telling me to let him go so my brother wouldn't suffer, and I had my cousin telling me it was OK to break my brother's ribs and chest cavity—just wait on God. So I prayed.

I decided to call the doctor back, but when I did, she wasn't in her office. So I left a message. I told her to keep my brother on life support and to please resuscitate him if his heart failed. I wanted them to break bones or whatever else it would take to save my brother, no matter how ugly it would get. If he died, at least we'd know we did everything we could to save him.

The doctor called me back and agreed to honor my decision, and I got on the next plane to Los Angeles to see my brother. When I got there, a friend of my brother's was there. She was a counselor, and she and my brother were very close. Other close family members were there also. When I came in, everybody cleared a path and gave me space. Everyone could always see the connection and strong bond between my brother and me. The counselor was moved by that. She came over and asked me what I was going to do. I told her we were going to let it happen naturally.

The doctor came in and asked to speak with me privately. She said, "Mr. Thomas, you don't want to go through this. If his heart fails, we have to break his chest cavity to get to his heart. I know death is hard, but it's a part of life. If you'd just sign this now, you'd really be helping your brother. If this were my brother, I would do it. That's what I would do." I said, "Yeah, I'm just going to let God do it. Whatever happens, just put it on God. It's in his hands. The way you explained it on the phone made me initially agree with you, but I believe you know that I was caught up in your concerns about breaking the bones. But it doesn't matter. Whatever it takes, I want him to live at all costs." I could tell she was disappointed with my decision, but it was firm and final.

My brother was in a coma for eight days. I was staying with a friend in Hermosa Beach at the time. I would go out there every day. On the eighth day, I remember getting a call before I got to the hospital. It was my mother. My heart stopped for a second before I heard her say, "Tony woke up. He's talking to us." I said, "Mom, no!" She said, "Yeah, child. Oooooh, ain't God good?"

I remember believing strongly that he would come out of it, and I had decided not to think about any funeral arrangements. I felt if I had gotten a suit that he would have died. When I got the news from Mom, I felt like I was in another world. I know God is amazing, but there was no rhyme or reason for him waking up. It was truly a miracle.

I went to the hospital, and there he was, holding court as only he could do. He said, "Uh, Ernie. I heard that you told the doctor to take me off of life support if my heart gave out." I said, "Oh, yeah. But I changed my decision." He said, "OK, because

I wouldn't have done that to you." He was just joking with me, but I felt bad. However, the important thing was I corrected it.

The doctor was crying like a baby. She was beside herself. She said there was no explanation for his waking up. He just woke up. But we knew it was divine. God is amazing! And He still does miracles.

So, I asked Tony if he remembered anything before waking up. He said he remembered going down a dark, winding road. On the side of the road were people who had died, and they were walking toward him. It was nighttime, and he heard a voice in the darkness asking him if he wanted to live or die. The voice said, "If you're not afraid of dying, I'll let you live." He said he told the voice, "I'm not afraid." All of a sudden, things shifted, and he was now going in the opposite direction. As he was moving along, light came into view and grew brighter as he moved further in that direction. In this direction, he saw people who were still alive, and they were walking toward him. Then he woke up.

I still thank God for that experience all the time. This is why I always tell people that I'm not the one to talk to about how bad a situation is, because I'm going to tell you that there is a solution. I'm not saying that it always has to be a miracle. But I believe it's God's will that we live and prosper. I'm extreme. I believe we're always supposed to get well, but we don't have the type of faith that Jesus talked about in Matthew 21:21 — that if we say to a mountain be moved, that it will be moved. Very few of us have that type of faith. But that is how it's supposed to be. And I know some disagree with that. Some believe that it can't be helped if it's God's will. I don't buy it, not of an illness.

If someone dies of natural causes, that person just moves on. But an illness that Christ has given us authority over should not lead to death. It's hard to face the fact that we just don't have faith. My grandmother didn't live long after she had a stroke. I didn't have the type of faith that could see my grandmother healed. That's the way it is. Seeing this miracle brought us all to tears. Just the thought of losing my brother was overwhelming to me. I was the older brother. I thought I should die first.

My brother was HIV positive. He had gotten pneumonia and had an allergic reaction to some medication they had given him, and that led to him slipping into a coma. My brother now felt that he had been granted a new life — that he'd been born again. He told us he had decided to live his new life to the fullest. He was no longer going to do what others wanted him to do; he was now going to do what he wanted to do.

Another one of his close friends was there that day. All of a sudden, she asked him, "Anton, how did you become gay?" We were all stunned that she would ask him that question at that moment. He had almost died. And while I knew she was grateful that he was alive, it seemed as if her question was saying "you wouldn't be HIV positive, or you wouldn't have had an allergic reaction to medication, or you wouldn't have been in a coma if you weren't gay." But why was she asking that now? My brother looked at her and said, "Your husband." She said, "What?" He said, "You heard me. Your husband is the reason why." He had never shared that with anybody. But he told us that her husband had approached him years ago. Everyone who knew my brother knew he was not a liar. His friend, overcome by embarrassment, stormed out of the room and left the hospital.

After I returned to New York, one of my brother's friends told me that Anton wanted to become a transgender female. He said, "He doesn't want to tell you." I said, "He doesn't want to tell me? Of all people, he should know that I'm going to love him no matter what. I can't believe he told you first." He said, "Yeah, he's told your mother and your sister." I was surprised. I thought Mom would have been the last person he told because Mom is a Baptist to the ninth power.

Anton finally called me. He started the conversation with a lot of small talk that meant nothing. Then he said, "Oh, when you come back to LA, I have something to talk to you about." I said, "Oh, OK. Are you sure you don't want to tell me now?" He said, "Well…" I said, "You know I love you unconditionally. What could you tell me that would stop me from loving you? There's nothing you can tell me that will make me stop loving you. So, shoot." He said, "Well, your brother is going to be your sister." I said, "Come again?" He laughed and said, "Your brother is going to be your sister," trying to make a joke out of it. I said, "Ohhh…" He said, "Yeah, after coming back to life after being given up for dead, I've decided that I want to live my life according to what I want and not what anybody else wants for me. I don't care about what people think anymore. This is something I've thought about, and I don't want to shy away from it now. I want to go all the way." I said, "Well, I wish you wouldn't. I'm not saying that out of hate. You're gay, and we've accepted that. Now you have a desire to be a woman? I don't understand that. I'm not saying that your desire isn't legitimate. I just don't understand why you have to go through that, especially since you've been through a health crisis already. Is that going to endanger your health?" He said, "No, this is something that will make me the happiest I've ever been. I'll be really happy to be the person I've always felt I was meant to be." I said, "OK. I just want to go on record as saying that I wish you wouldn't. But, I'll be there for you." And he thanked me.

Not long after that conversation, he started taking female hormones. But he did not want to be a complete woman. He didn't want his penis removed because sometimes people who do it commit suicide The doctors did say that taking the hormone shots, with his health being in the fragile state it was in, was not a good idea. But he said he'd rather die being authentically who he was than to live a lie. All I could do was be there. I wasn't happy about it, but I wanted him to be happy with himself.

In the summer of that year, my brother said he was ready for the transgender ceremony. It was going to be at Bishop Dean's church. He's a gay minister, with a large LGBTQ congregation. Bishop Dean was the first minister to give Aids and HIV tests in the church because most people were in denial about it, particularly Black people. Then, when Eazy-E died, people welcomed him and sent donations because he was trying to save lives. And straight ministers weren't trying to do that. They didn't want to touch it at all. He said, "Look, people need to get tested to see if they need help, and to stop having sex if they're infected."

I received many calls from both Christians and Muslims, saying, "Brother, I know you love your brother, but you should not be at that ceremony. It is an abomination. He's going to hell." My Muslim brothers said, "Give up on him. Let him go." There was no love at all.

There is a high suicide rate among transgender people, particularly because their families desert them. You don't have to agree with what a person is doing, but you can still be there. We all need love and support. Being honest and saying, "I hate what you're doing, but I'm here because I love you" is so much better than banishing a person from your life. That's not love. And that's why I couldn't understand why my Christian and Muslim friends didn't understand.

Surprisingly, my brother's gay friends were also prejudice against transgender people. There were certain gay friends that I knew would be there. But he said, "No, they're not coming." They don't like that. They think a man should look like a man." I said, "Even though they're gay like you're gay, only you're becoming transgender? They can't be there to support you?" He said, "No." That was a revelation to me. There's prejudice everywhere, even within the LGBTQ community.

I went to the ceremony alone. My mother did not go. She loved my brother, but she couldn't do it. And I understood. This was all foreign to her. But I did not want my brother to commit suicide because the one person he loved above all was saying, "I ain't coming." I was nervous and uneasy because this was uncharted territory to me. I didn't even know a ceremony like that existed, or that a church like that existed. But my brother needed me, and I was going to be there.

When I arrived at the church, it is packed. I couldn't find a seat, so I stood in the back. The bishop started by talking about what the ceremony means and saying a few other things. Then I heard him say "formerly Anton Thomas and now Toni Sue Farrell." I don't recall exactly how he said it all, but that's the gist of it. Then a man and a woman sang "A Whole New World," from the *Beauty and the Beast* soundtrack. Everybody was clapping. My brother was dressed in a bridal gown with a bridal headdress and veil. He looked like a woman—makeup and lipstick, the works. I was standing there observing this and all the while thinking about that little baby that had come into the world on Thanksgiving Day in 1960. Now, there he was, being presented as born again—reborn in this way.

I watched him as he came down the aisle and passed by. He was so focused, and he looked amazing. My brother had always been handsome. He turned and went back to the altar in the front of the church. At this point, I'm thinking, *"Oh, my God. What next?"* But I put on a smile. I didn't want him to know I was stressed. I wanted to really be there for him.

When he got to the altar, his "mother," an elder transgender lady, and her husband were waiting for him. They handed him his certificate, and the Bishop said a few more words, and my brother officially became Toni Sue Farrell.

Then the Bishop asked, "Do you have any folks here?" My brother told him I was there. I waved, and the Bishop invited me to come up to the altar. So, I did. I greeted them and congratulated them all, and I told my brother that I was happy for him. Then I stood aside as they took pictures. One of the bishops leaned in to me and said, "Look, brother, I know you're uncomfortable. It's understandable. But it means so much to your brother that you're here. Just know that Bishop Dean has the support of many who help him financially to test and help people in South Central." That was reassuring.

My brother said, "Let's take a photo!" *A photo!* I said, "Eh-hey. Yeah, alright." Then I took a picture with my brother, hoping all the while that the *National Enquirer* was not here. I could just see it: the photo and the write up about my marriage to a transgender woman.

Then I talked to his "mother." She was very kind. She said, "Don't worry. I'm going to take good care of your brother. He's part of our family now."

My brother often entered many contests. He'd impersonate Patti LaBelle and other celebrity singers and actresses. One day he wanted to stop by to get some money. I forgot that he would be wearing a dress. So, when he came by, I honestly didn't recognize him. I saw a woman in a green dress. I was concerned about him coming into South Central, but he really looked like a woman. I don't think anyone would have suspected that he wasn't a woman. He came in, and I gave him some money. My friend and her girlfriend immediately asked, "Who was that lady?" I said, "That's my brother. They thought I was lying. I said, "That's Anton."

Anton was always fashionable, and he knew how to do hair. Women would pay him 100 dollars or whatever he charged to do their hair. He never went to school for anything. He just had natural gifts. He had the gift of gab. He could talk to any- and everyone. If you gave him something to do, he could learn how to do it with little effort. And people always called him for advice. That was all the time, and he loved it. He would give them that hard-core, tough love.

And when he needed to talk, he'd call me. He called me one night after he had gone over to see our mother. He said our mother and sister had given him a certain look, as if they were mad at him. It's the look we often give our loved ones, when they're not looking, that replaces the fake smile we provide when we don't want to upset them by letting our true feelings show.

I said, "Now, you know for a fact that your mother loves you and would die for you. But she is a southern, Black, Baptist woman, baptized at nine years old in the Mississippi River. If you think she's going to accept this whole-heartedly, that ain't happening right now. It might not ever happen. She's going to love you. But she ain't ever gonna say, 'Oh, you know what? I'm so happy you're a transgender woman.' You're expecting something that's just not reality. And that goes for your sister, too. She loves you. But you gotta understand that." I could hear him crying. I said, "Don't cry, Tony." You have to allow people to be where they are—even the cousins who act ugly toward you and hate you. Just ignore it because they're acting out of disapproval of your choice. It's something that disgusts them. They just can't wrap their minds around it at all. But you definitely have to understand they love you, but they're also saying 'I'm not comfortable with this.' You go around your mother with a dress and heels on, and she remembers that boy that was in her womb for nine months. He came here a boy, was always a boy, and all of a sudden, now he's a woman. Think about that. That's a lot for her to handle. And yet she's not ever gonna say,

'Don't come to my house; you're not my child.' She'll never say that, so she'll fake it until you look away because she's still asking, 'Why?'" That's the thing he could not understand — that people were not going to be in agreement with it just because he thought they should.

There's always going to be prejudices in the world. As people, we will always choose not to like someone just because of race, gender, ethnicity, sexual orientation, or whatever. In most instances, we know that it is horrible, but often we feel it is justified. I know a White lady who hated all Black people. I am friends with her son. She told me that her nephew's best friend was Black, and he killed her nephew. So she didn't want me to be around her son. She just didn't trust Black people. But it's things like this that we must try to understand. It doesn't mean it's right, but there is usually a reason. It's where a person comes from and what that person has been exposed to that makes that person who he or she is. You gotta understand where a person is coming from. But my brother never fully got that.

A few months later, my brother passed away. I was still staying with Inez in South Central. He had called me because he wanted me to take him to the doctor, but I had not gotten the message. So my niece had picked him up. I guess my niece and my mother took him to the hospital. When I spoke with him on the phone, he said, "Yeah, I'm good. I'm here now." I said, "Ah, man. That's good. At least you're there. I'll be by there later." He sounded great — full of spirit. Then my sister called me a few minutes later and said Anton had died. She told me they had given him a shot. I don't think they deliberately kill people in hospitals, but I do believe the staff that was caring for him that day is responsible for his death. I can't prove it, but I believe it. There is so much going on in emergency rooms, and sometimes people make mistakes that cost lives.

I don't know what they gave him, but my sister went off and said they had killed him. I had just talked to my baby brother. And literally moments later, they said we'd lost him. I remember standing in the living room when I heard the news. I try not to cry when I'm around people. I keep my tears between me and God. But it couldn't be helped then. The tears came. Ali's daughter Maryum "May May" Ali was there, along with Inez. They hugged me and consoled me. I thank God that I didn't have to bear that alone. There are no words to describe the grief I felt in that moment. I wouldn't wish it on my worst enemy. I had heard my brother's voice so clear, "Hey, I'm here. Everything's fine." And then he was gone.

We had the funeral at Bishop Dean's church. People from many different races, religions, and cultures, and different walks of life came to my brother's funeral. I had no idea his life had touched so many people. Many of them had stories about how he had helped them in some way. There were so many people that I didn't get a chance to speak to.

He requested to be buried in a dress—one of his dresses, with makeup, wig, and his new name. So, we buried him as Toni Sue Farrell. My mother had a hard time dealing with that. But I said, "Mom, we have to honor his wishes and the way he wanted to be remembered.

About a week later, I was driving on the freeway, and it hit me—my brother was gone. Memories of the past flooded my mind like a movie. The reality sank in and hit me so hard, I had to pull over. I said, "God, I can't do this. I can't. I can't go on. I just can't go on. My baby's gone. You know, God. I know you understand that I'm having a difficult time here, Lord." I said things that I hate to hear people say. I believe it's OK to express grief, but we can and must live without our loved ones when they pass on. We have to rest in God, knowing that he will give us strength to carry on and be there for others.

I'm thankful to God that my brother's passing is still not completely real to me. Anton has been gone since 1995, but no one, not even my mother and sister, have ever heard me express my grief. . I just don't do that. Every now and then, I post a picture on Facebook on Throwback Thursdays, with the caption "Gone too soon." But I still haven't come to grips with the fact that he's not here. I am aware that he is no longer here, but I cannot totally accept it.

*****

In 1999, I moved in with my mother and sister in Glendale, California. That's when the blessings really flowed. I did mostly plays. But then, as God would have it, out of left field came *Everybody Hates Chris*. Friends in the business were telling me that Chris Rock was trying to get in touch with me. I thought, *"Yeah, right! Sure he is!"* But I soon found out that he was. He and his co-creator, Ali LeRoi, wanted me to audition for the show. Initially, it was for a different role, and it was only one line. There were a lot of other actors auditioning for the part, so I really didn't think I'd get it. I came in, did my line, and left. But I got a call a few days later. I had gotten the part. After that, they called me and offered be a recurring role, Mr. Omar. I didn't even have to audition. I had met Chris once before. But I had no idea that he and Ali would create a role specifically for me. There are so many other superstars that have told me they were going to do this and that, but they never did. But Chris, whom I barely knew, was thinking about me.

Chris had grown up watching the show. And out of that love he created Mr. Omar. I am grateful because the show introduced me to a whole new audience. *Everybody Hates Chris* was huge, especially overseas in Europe and Brazil. Now I have a whole new following that know nothing about *What's Happening!!* and don't care about *What's Happening!!* All they know is that they love Mr. Omar. Just look at God.

I did that show for four years, and I loved every minute of it. Tachina was my muse. She made me want to be funny. And I loved Terry. He was always letting me know, "Man, I love you so much. You know how much we love you?" Even the kids treated me with so much honor and respect. They used to say they hoped I'd be in every episode. I remember Tachina saying on the first day, "We should have him on every episode, ya'll." I felt truly blessed.

Ali LeRoi was a big help to me, and he still is. He's such a creative person. I really appreciate how he could always read me. He knew when I didn't like certain lines, and he was always open to what I had to say. I had to adjust to not having a live audience. I was used to hearing laughter. I went to Terry one day and said, "Man, it's tough not knowing if the audience gets it." He said, "Oh, you're funny. Trust me, because if you weren't, they'd tell you."

I always felt so honored and fortunate to be a part of the show because they didn't need me. I really appreciated their love and admiration. Ali LeRoi once said, "Ernie, we didn't hire you out of charity. If you didn't bring anything to the table, as much as we admire you, we never would have hired you." That was good to know. I later found out from someone else that it's called branding — that I have a brand. Who knew? And you have to capitalize on your brand to have a following. My name brings X amount of people to watch that show after all these years. I did only thirty-one maybe thirty-three episodes. But they are aired a lot, thank God.

Things got a little slow after *Everybody Hates Chris*. I mainly did guest spots here and there, and a lot of personal appearances. I thank God that in the forty years I've been in the business I've never taken a job in another profession. Everything I've done has revolved around my acting career. Now, I went through some lean times because money got scarce, but that's when God would send a big residual check. My faith has definitely grown.

Although I had started visiting churches again, I didn't want to belong to any one church. My primary source of ministry came from watching ministers on TBN and YouTube. When my mother was ill and slipped into a coma, the doctors were telling me it didn't look good. I remember putting TBN on twenty-four/seven in that hospital room. I told the nurses that it had to stay on at all times. Although her mind wasn't awake, her spirit was. I put the speakers by her head. And I only allowed people with faith to see her. I didn't want anybody crying around her. I had those people of strong faith there, and we'd hold hands and pray around her.

The doctors met with me to caution me about being optimistic. I said, "Doctors, I appreciate you. And I really do appreciate your intelligence and professionalism. You have credentials, but I believe in the supernatural power of Jesus Christ to heal. I have seen it before, and I expect a healing in this room. I expect my mother to walk out of this hospital." Those four doctors looked at me like I was an alien. I knew we weren't on the same page. They weren't bad guys, but they didn't speak that language. But I couldn't let them impose their negativity on me.

They did a battery of tests and had a specialist examine her. They initially thought that pancreatitis was the cause of her condition. But it wasn't that. Then it was something else and something else. Finally, they said, "Oh, it's the gall bladder." So, they had to put her under anesthesia. They were worried about her because of her age, and she had congenital heart failure. Then they warned me of the risks involved. I thought, *"Oh, here we go again.* So, I said, "I have to pray on that."

I went home and called each of my friends that were doctors and asked them what they thought. They all advised me to go for it. It was worth the risk. I was thankful that I had doctors as friends who could tell me the real deal. Mom survived the surgery. Then she needed a blood transfusion because the bile from her gall bladder was in her blood. They did the blood transfusion, and Mom finally woke up. She had been in a coma for almost a month, in the intensive care.

It took a while for Mom to recover. She had to go to another hospital for rehabilitation. She had to learn how to talk and swallow again. She had to learn how to walk and raise her hands. It was like teaching a new-born baby. And it was very tough on me. I was brave by day, but I cried every night. I was still believing that Mom would get through this, but it was a very trying time. Her enthusiasm was amazing, even at eighty-two years old. They had to tell her to get her rest because she wouldn't slow down. She wanted to get out of there. When I looked at her, my heart would swell with so much pride. I'd come from a strong woman who had passed that strength on to me. Mom is doing well to this day. She has a great team of doctors and a mighty God on her side. Her sickness was the toughest thing I'd ever gone through. But the Lord let me know that I had to go through it, yet he'd never leave me alone. His grace sustained me and helped me through it.

One Sunday in 2016, I decided to go to West Angeles Church of God in Christ, and Bishop Blake was on fire. I was wondering why I was feeling at home there. I knew I wasn't going to join a church. That just wasn't going to happen. Then I came back the next Sunday and the next Sunday and the next. One of the ushers welcomed me at the door one Sunday and said, "Brother, it's about time you joined us, isn't it?" I said, "Brother, you know I'm fighting it. I'm fighting it hard, but I don't know." He said, "You might as well come on in." I tried to fight it, but I knew God had led me there. I knew all about the celebrities that attend, but that doesn't mean anything to me. I would never go to a church because someone there is popular. The only star is Jesus Christ. There is no other star.

Attending West Angeles is like returning home to where it all began. I'm so thankful that I have a place where I can go to praise and thank him for saving my life. When I told my mom

I was thinking about joining, she was surprised, but I knew she was happy. I have members of my family who look at me as if I need an endorsement or something, as if they're not quite sure I'm born again. But God spoke to me, and no one can tell me who I am in Christ. I have a relationship with him, and no one has anything to do with it.

There are some Muslim brothers who have chosen never to speak to me again just because I'm back in the church. This one particular Muslim brother and I were very close, and my mother told me that he'd stop calling once he found out I was back in the church. I didn't want to believe her, but she was right. Another brother said, "Oh, I'm so sorry to hear that," when I told him.

We are all God's children, and he loves us unconditionally. Embracing that love and having a revelation of it helps us to, in turn, love others as he has commanded us to do. It all comes down to love. When we judge, condemn, and shun one another, that is the complete opposite of how we are to show God's love. As God's children, covered in his grace, we should be true representations of his unconditional love and mercy. I praise God for showing me his supernatural power. Thought the hardships and pain, he kept me and drew me closer to him. Then he blessed me with amazing opportunities. Those also were miracles. And through those experiences, my faith grew stronger. There is nothing God cannot do.

CHAPTER TEN

RICHES

A long with witnessing the miracle of my mom's healing, I also saw God heal three other friends after they had been given their last rights. Seeing and experiencing God's supernatural power is worth more than all the silver and gold in this world. True and lasting peace, love, joy, and riches come from God.

This revelation has helped me to get in tune with God and stay there through daily prayer and meditation, and by reading and listening to God's Word, studying God's Word, and listening to ministers who teach on God's Word. I'm constantly listening to sermons and gospel songs because there's so much in the world that is poisoning our spirits.

With all that's going on in life, we constantly encounter spiritual wickedness that we cannot see. Our eyes and ears are constantly bombarded with interactions through social media, TV programs, movies, billboards, and other means of communication that can weigh us down, both mentally and spiritually, without even knowing it. So, I try to keep myself fed with spiritual food that I know will strengthen my spirit and increase my faith. No matter how long we have been believers, we can never take our spiritual health for granted. We must fortify our spirits daily.

As we grow spiritually, we must also die daily. We must ask God to crucify our fleshly desires and eliminate selfishness. Being selfish and perpetuating selfish attitudes take us further away from all that God has for us. Relying on God's help to deliver us from negative thoughts and deeds helps us to stay in his will, and stay equipped to stand against the negative forces that try to come against us.

As believers, we must also pray for one another. We have become so divided in the world. Everyone has his or her own thoughts, opinions, and interpretations about God and what he has said. Instead of being one unified body with a common goal, we are fragment.

But what would happen if we came together, prayed together, and worked together. If we all desire to see God honored through our service to mankind, imagine how powerful and effective we could be to that end if we truly loved and respected one another. I may not agree with everything you believe or say, but we can agree to disagree in love and work for the greater good. The common thread is love.

Our children are looking for answers. When they find more love and acceptance in the world than they do in our places of worship, there is still much work to do. We can find young kids, nine and ten years old, dealing drugs, trying to get their mothers into a better situation. We have young men joining gangs because they need to feel accepted and loved. We have young girls being sold for sex and others getting pregnant because they want someone to love. Why is this happening when there are thousands of churches in our neighborhoods? Is the devil more effective?

If people are afraid to come through our doors out of the fear of being ostracized and rejected, things must change. We have serious issues and major problems that are plaguing our world, and many are crying out for help. We don't have time to be concerned with who's been baptized in this way or that, the color of one's skin, or the clothes one wears. It's time to roll up our sleeves and make a difference in this world. We can't stick our heads in the sand and stay confined to our own circles of influence. We must be the hands and feet of God in the earth, spreading his light and love.

I always say we never go through something for nothing. As I said before, our God is purposeful, and he uses everything we experience for our good. God has blessed me to go places I thought I'd never go and meet people that I am truly grateful to have loved and known. It is my sincere desire that something I've said or done has impacted your life in a real and meaning-ful way and given you deeper insight in your own personal reflection of who you are, what you've done, and what God still has for you to do.

I've seen my share of up and downs, as all of us have. We all have a story, and no one can tell your story better than you. I've been to hell and back and recently God revealed to me that the real hero in my life is me. I tell people all the time: "Be your own hero." When I rewind the tape and reflect on almost be-ing aborted; being molested; being bullied; being an asthmatic; having no father; experiencing racism; being on welfare; being addicted to drugs and alcohol; being in the lion's den with drug dealers and many guns; being in hotel rooms alone—freebasing and not knowing if I would survive through the night; suffering religious persecution from family and friends, but still holding on to the promise of God, Ernest Thomas is my hero. When I look back at myself and at all God did for me, I see a man walking tall, with his back straight, despite not having toilet paper or a dime in his pocket, at one point in time. But I still walked as if I owned the world, because I still knew God.

There are many great people who have done, and are doing, remarkable things in this world. And we should celebrate them for using their gifts to add beauty to the world. But we must walk in our own calling and continuously depend on God's grace and anointing to help us make our own mark in the world.

Life isn't perfect; God never promised that it would be. So we must celebrate the good times and press through the bad so that we can show others how God brought us out. No matter what we go through, it's an absolute fact that we will make it through. The key is to keep your mouth shut when it comes to expressing any negativity or doubts about your heart's desires or dreams. Always speak the sacrifice of praise. Your feelings most of the time are traitors to your soul–especially if they aren't aligned with what God is leading and directing you to do.

When I first got to Hollywood, there were times, while lying in that dingy hotel bed, that I had doubts and fears. But I only expressed them to Jesus. I never spoke it to anyone, not even my mother, not even my friend Jake. I decided it would be God and me alone. And that was sufficient to win. Today I believe my latter days will be greater than my past. Yes, I appreciate *What's Happening!!* and all the past television shows and movies I've done, but I know the best is yet to come. In the past few years, I have performed in at least eight sold-out theater shows at the Wilshire Ebell Theater. I was blessed to be cast by two prolific playwrights, Brandi Burks Kesselman and Don B. Welch. On Easter Sunday, I starred opposite the great Loretta Devine, Christian Keyes, and Kiki Haynes in a live theater movie *Lost Souls Café,* written by Don Welch. It was a huge hit on TV One. Independent filmmakers like Mykel Shannon Jenkins cast me in very challenging roles in *Two Wolves, The Gods,* and *The Chosen One.* And Jean-Claude La Marre cast me in *Chocolate City* and *Chocolate City 2.* These films will be seen this fall or next year. I received great reviews for my performance as a stroke victim in *Paroled,* written and directed by Sal Martino. A scene from the film was uploaded to YouTube by one of my protégés, and I got a lot of hits and respect, especially from the hip hop community. That scene has helped me get four dramatic roles that I never would've been considered for.

I also have starred in several critically acclaimed short films. I'm reinventing myself and empowering my brand. I have done great guest starring roles on *Workaholics* and *Veep.* I was also chosen by Oscar award-winning writer and director John Ridley for his new series *Presence.*

I no longer stress about any of projects. They may or may not be a hit, but I do know God has great things in store for me because God never lies, He always keeps his promises. I'm always advising or consulting new artists because I want to pay it forward. That was my promise to God on the plane when I was on my way to Hollywood, and I intend to keep it.

Never think your gift is too small or that your gift doesn't matter. It matters, because you matter. And God has placed something in you that no one else can contribute to this world but you. So, yes, be your own hero and celebrate your place in this world.

Like many others, I've had my share of ups and downs — joy and sorrow. But, as the old hymn says, through it all, I've learned to trust in Jesus; I've learned to trust in God. With his help, I've been blessed beyond measure. For that I am thankful. But as Paul said, I consider everything else worthless when compared with the value of knowing Christ. Without him I am nothing. The richest man doesn't have all the money in the world; he has a loving and awesome God. Material riches fade, but God's rewards are eternal. There are three things that will last forever: faith, hope, and love. And the greatest of these is love. I love you eternally, my friend. God bless you.

44644113R00098

Made in the USA
Middletown, DE
13 June 2017